HOUSE OF HORRORS

Nick Arnold & Tony De Saulles

SCHOLASTIC

www.horrible-science.co.uk
www.nickarnold-website.com
www.tonydesaulles.co.uk

Scholastic Children's Books
Euston House,
24 Eversholt Street,
London NW1 1DB, UK

A division of Scholastic Ltd
London ~ New York ~ Toronto ~ Sydney ~ Auckland
Mexico City ~ New Delhi ~ Hong Kong

Editorial Project Manager: Jill Sawyer
Assistant Editor: Corinne Lucas
Indexer: Caroline Hamilton

First published in the UK by Scholastic Ltd, 2012
This edition published 2013

ISBN 978 1407 13521 2

Printed and bound by Tien Wah Press Pte. Ltd, Singapore

2 4 6 8 10 9 7 5 3 1

CONTENTS

WELCOME TO THE HOUSE OF HORRORS!

Lightning flashes and thunder rumbles. The rain pours and the wind howls around the creepy castle. As midnight strikes, something crawls in search of human blood…

Is your home this scary? "NO WAY!" you squeak. "My home is safe as houses!"
Well, you're wrong. Once you've read this book you'll know the Horrible Truth. Every home has hidden horrors! Lurking in dark corners there could be…

Grease and grime and scabby dead skin.

Creeping, crawling bugs, foul flies and sinister spiders.

Snot, spots and fingernails.

And that's just the sickening start. With a microscope you can spot millions of microbes.* They're much more tiny – and much more scary! You'll be shocked at what's making itself at home in your home. In fact your home just won't feel the same!

*microbe = microscopic life-form

So have you got the guts to search for sickening secrets in your home? We've got a sickening story to inspire you. It's about mad scientist Baron Frankenstein. The Baron made two children from bits of body. And now he's invited three scientists to hunt for hidden horrors in his creepy castle.

HOME IS WHERE THE HEART IS.

Barmy Baron

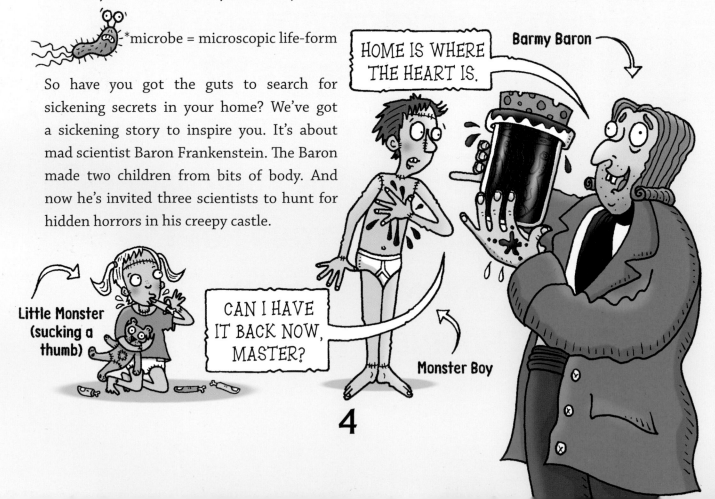

Little Monster (sucking a thumb)

CAN I HAVE IT BACK NOW, MASTER?

Monster Boy

4

So where did the Baron get the body bits? Hmm – just don't ask! The scientists will be using a shrinking machine to study tiny terrors close up. Now I don't know if they'll live to tell the tale. But one thing is certain. Science is coming home – and it's going to be HORRIBLE!

Feeling brave? It's time to open up the House of Horrors!

THAT SHRINKING FEELING

The scientists arrive at the castle. But before they start they need a volunteer to test their shrinking machine. So would you volunteer to shrink to the size of an atom? Or would you rather have your ears twisted until they're about to come off? The Baron bribes Junior with a choccie bar…

The shrinking scientists in… How low can you get?

0.5 mm = grain of salt.

I'M BEING A-SALTED!

2.5 mm long = Now he's the size of a grain of rice.

EEK!

8 mm = He's no bigger than a baked bean.

EH?

60 microns = Paramecium microbe. Junior is now too small for the Shrinking Scientists to see.

URGH! IT'S SLIME TIME!

30 microns = a dead human skin cell.

NOW I'VE GOT DISGUSTING DANDRUFF!

4 microns = a yeast. This microbe makes bread dough rise.

DOH!

6.5 nanometres = haemoglobin molecule. Haemoglobin carries oxygen in your red blood cells.

I'M SEEING RED!

30 nanometres – ATISSHOOO! Junior is splatted by a cold virus.

SPLOOP!

Viruses break into cells and hijack the DNA codes. They order the cell to make new viruses until it dies.

0.6 microns = E. coli. This bacterium (two or more are called bacteria) slithers in your guts.

URGH!

0.9 nanometres = glucose molecule. Your cells turn this type of sugar into energy.

SWEET!

0.375 nanometres = carbon atom. It forms diamonds, coal and pencil lead.

VZZ! VZZ! VZZ! VZZ!

YIKES!

0.275 nanometres = water molecule.

GET ME OUTTA HERE!

IT WET MY PANTS!

What's that? You've absolutely got to have a shrinking machine for your birthday? Er, sorry – I made it up. But there's a real machine you can try. It's on the next page...

MAD ABOUT MICROSCOPES

Scientists use microscopes to study terribly tiny things. Stuff like ant brains, little-brother brains, teacher brains, mouldy microbes, that kind of thing. Here's how they work...

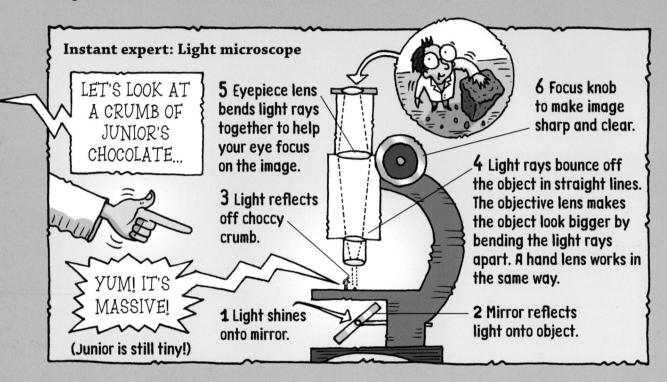

Instant expert: Light microscope

LET'S LOOK AT A CRUMB OF JUNIOR'S CHOCOLATE...

5 Eyepiece lens bends light rays together to help your eye focus on the image.

3 Light reflects off choccy crumb.

6 Focus knob to make image sharp and clear.

4 Light rays bounce off the object in straight lines. The objective lens makes the object look bigger by bending the light rays apart. A hand lens works in the same way.

YUM! IT'S MASSIVE!

(Junior is still tiny!)

1 Light shines onto mirror.

2 Mirror reflects light onto object.

Modern microscopes use a camera linked to a computer screen. You can print cool pictures. But the shrinking scientists want to check out the cold virus from page 7. Trouble is, the virus is even smaller than waves of light. This means it's too tiny to be seen with an ordinary microscope. Fortunately the scientists have brought an electron microscope...

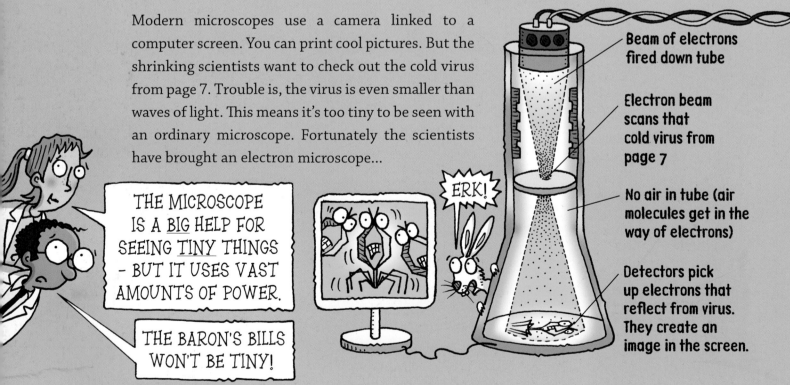

THE MICROSCOPE IS A BIG HELP FOR SEEING TINY THINGS – BUT IT USES VAST AMOUNTS OF POWER.

THE BARON'S BILLS WON'T BE TINY!

ERK!

Beam of electrons fired down tube

Electron beam scans that cold virus from page 7

No air in tube (air molecules get in the way of electrons)

Detectors pick up electrons that reflect from virus. They create an image in the screen.

The shrinking scientists want to study my cold virus. It takes the scientists ages to prepare the virus. It has to be painted gold to reflect electrons and freeze-dried to so it won't be destroyed in the airless tube. Then Monster Boy wants to try the microscope treatment. Is he a teeny bit crazy … or a great big bit crazy?

The shrinking scientists in… A little spot of bother

But the experiment goes a tiny bit wrong…

Monster Boy is rescued just in time. But then the scientists spot some squishy snot up the Baron's left nostril …

BACTERIA BEHAVING BADLY

The Baron's snot is squirming with bacteria. Fancy a peek?

CHOMP! SPLURP!

Bacterium feeding on snot and scabby skin flakes

Tasty blob of snot

Bacteria are smaller than cells

Slime coat stops bacterium from drying out

Outer wall holds bacterium in shape whilst letting in food and water

YUM! YUM!

MUNCH! SPLOOP! SLURP! SPLIT!

Flagellum – a tiny swimming tail. Other bacteria have swimming hairs – just imagine if you could swim by waving your hair!

Bacteria can divide every 20 minutes.

No nucleus for DNA. Bacteria happily swap DNA to make new and revolting varieties of bacteria.

Could you be a bacteriologist*?

*back-teer-re-ollo-gist = scientist who studies bacteria.

1 What's the weight of the E. coli bacteria in your guts?

a) 100 grams

b) 0.0001 grams

2 If you scooped your skin bacteria into a slimy ball how big would it be?

a) Smaller than a pea

b) The size of a table tennis ball

3 How many bacteria are there in the world?

a) 100 billion – but they don't stay still long enough to count.

b) 5 nonillion.

UGH! YOU'RE MAKING ME ITCH!

Answers:

1 a) 100 grams. That's nearly a pot of yogurt. Anyone fancy e-coli-flavour yog?

2 a) If you said **b)** you need a bath NOW! In fact your body bacteria outnumber your cells TEN TO ONE!

3 b) It's only a scientist's guess. To make a nonillion you multiply 10 x 10 x 10 ... then do it 27 more times. (It's brain-bogglingly BIG!)

So how do bacteria get around? I mean, they can't ride a bike. In fact we give them a lift. Just look at Monster Boy...

Pie not properly cooked. It's squelching with bacteria.

SQUELCH!

WHAT YOU LOOKING AT?

MONSTER BOY HAVE YOU WASHED YOUR HANDS?

WHICH ONE MASTER?

CHOMP!

SQUIRM!

Hands not washed after visit to the loo. Micro poo blobs oozing with germs.

Bacteria squirming between teeth

Putrid pants full of germs

Monster boy is crawling with germs. By the way, you might like to know that a germ is any microscopic thing that causes disease – including bacteria and viruses. So you're scared of bacteria? And you'll never kiss the cat again? Well, pull yourself together! You've lived with bacteria for years and they haven't killed you. And some bacteria are GOOD for you! Read this if you don't believe me...

● You're *covered* in skin bacteria. At least there's no room for harmful bacteria to move in.

● Gut bacteria block out the nasty germs in your guts and some make vitamin K. This helps your blood clot so it's definitely a good thing!

● Some bacteria hunt and munch other bacteria. So they're doing you a favour!

● Bacteria make tasty yogurt and cheese. Do you enjoy these edibles? Well, those microbes *must* be your mates... Unlike the vile viruses on the next page!

I HATE YO-GUTS.

THERE'S NO NEED TO GET PERSONAL!

VILE VIRUSES

You didn't invite viruses into your home but they're here anyway. And they're going to give you a really BAD time! Just imagine an army of tiny evil robots trying to take over your body. Vile viruses include chicken pox, cold sores and yellow fever.

BET YOU NEVER KNEW!

Yellow fever is as dangerous as potty-training an elephant. Along with aches, fever and black vomit, victims turn yellow. In the 1920s six scientists hunted separately for the virus. It killed them all!

I'M THE SIXTH SICK SCIENTIST, BLEURGH!

Back in the 1800s no-one knew how yellow fever spread. One US scientist working on the problem was Stubbins Ffirth (1784–1820)...

The secret diary of Stubbins Ffirth (aged 18)
For my first experiment I gave the dog a slice of bread. It's soaked in black vomit from a yellow fever victim. And guess what? The dog loves the sick! So I fed the cat on sick. She's fine too. So now it's my turn for the vomit treatment. This could prove interesting!

SLURP!

GULP!

SNIFF!

MUNCH!

You'll be grossed-out to hear that after scoffing sick, the strange scientist cut himself and poured vile vomit into his wounds. Then he did it TWENTY MORE TIMES. Then he sniffed and *drank* the sickening sick, and sampled poo and pee of fever patients just to make sure! Stupid Stubbins felt sure that you can't catch yellow fever. He was wrong. It's spread by mosquito bites and it's deadly if it gets into your blood. The bean-brained boffin was lucky not to catch the disease...

Hopefully you haven't got yellow fever at home so let's stick with a virus that we know (well, I do because it's up my nose). Can you believe some peculiar people volunteered to catch colds? It was their idea of a happy holiday!

FANCY A SNIFFLE?

Enjoy a virus vacation at the Common Cold Unit...

SNEEZE! COUGH!

C.C.U.

* Do your bit for science!
* Free hankies and medical treatment!
* Free flat (you'll share it with someone spluttering green phlegm all night!)
* Relax in a hot bath (then you have to sit in a draughty corridor and wear wet socks all day). Don't worry it's only an experiment!
* Enjoy a de-luxe VIP experiment - runny snot from a cold victim gets dripped into your nostrils!

Prices not to be sniffed at (but you might sniff a lot!)

HIGH TEMPERATURES GUARANTEED!

These experiments took place in Britain after 1945. The aim was to find out if being cold and wet made you catch colds. The results showed that you needed the virus to get a snotty nose. Talking about snot, most nasty cold effects are due to your body fighting the virus.

The Author

Extra blood flows to your nose. Water gets squeezed from the blood fluid. This makes snot runny.

Runny snot washes out the virus

I'VE DOT A GOLD!

Swollen veins cause that bunged-up feeling

You cough snot non-stop. The virus irritates your nose and makes you sneeze the virus everywhere until someone else catches it! In one 1950s experiment, scientists coloured snot with a glowing dye. Glowing snot from sneezes splattered over their walls and hands.

WHAT'S LURKING IN YOUR LIVING ROOM?

Your living room is where you relax and watch TV. Well, I hope it's less horrible than the Baron's loathsome living room!

1 Grimy windows. The Baron says the dirt stops people looking in. He gives them a wipe with pee-soaked rags. This is what people did in eighteenth-century America. What a potty idea!

2 Spit and germs. Every time you speak, spit splatters bacteria. Chances are there's dried dribble and gooey germs all over your living room.

3 Dried snot and fingernails. OH YUCK! Monster Boy picks his nose and bites his nails AT THE SAME TIME!

4 This cute little plaster beetle is just 2 mm long. Right now it's laying an egg.

5 Tasty mould is a plaster beetle banquet.

6 Ooooh dear – Little Monster's been sick. That'll teach her for scoffing dead flies!

14

7 Skullbox 10 with Monster Boy's Zombie-Zapper game. The grimy fingerprints are dried sweat and skin oils plus a bit of squished dirt.

8 Monster Boy's chewed-up cockroach-flavour chewing gum. It's squelching with spit, bacteria and dead mouth cells.

9 Speck of earwax. It's made of cerumen. This oily substance traps dead skin and bacteria. It plops out of your ear at embarrassing moments. Some people think that a blob of earwax in their mouth numbs toothache. It doesn't.

10 The carpet is jumping with dust mites. At 0.2 mm they're too small to see but you'll find them on page 72.

11 Woodworm hole. Inside, a furniture beetle larva is munching 5 cm of table leg per year. It pushes poo and wood dust out from its horrible hole.

12 Little Monster's Rattle-Bones game. Toddler toys are splattered with snotty dribble and germs.

13 Crunchy dead fly – you can discover more flies on page 54.

14 Look at this lovely dust – it's mostly dead human skin cells.

Instant expert - insects in your home

Here's everything you need to know about invading insects...

1 Awful insect anatomy

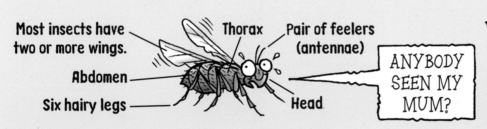

Most insects have two or more wings.

Thorax

Pair of feelers (antennae)

Abdomen

Six hairy legs

Head

ANYBODY SEEN MY MUM?

YEAH, SHE'S ABOVE THE FIREPLACE BY THE CANDLESTICK HOLDER ON PAGE 14!

2 Invading insect life-cycles

Some insect babies look like their parents and just grow bigger. Others have a life cycle like this...

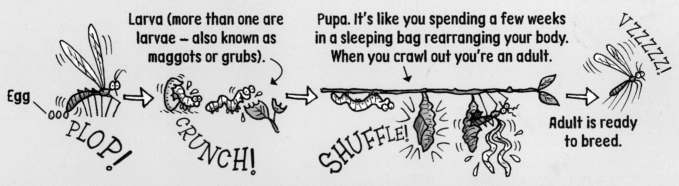

Egg

PLOP!

Larva (more than one are larvae – also known as maggots or grubs).

CRUNCH!

Pupa. It's like you spending a few weeks in a sleeping bag rearranging your body. When you crawl out you're an adult.

SHUFFLE!

VZZZZZ!

Adult is ready to breed.

Insects are horribly good at breeding. That's why they outnumber us humans 200 million to one!

A BREATH OF FRESH AIR?

PFWOAR! Hold onto your noses – Monster boy has let off a stink bomb!

Mind you, even if your living room smells as fresh as new pants it's still full of harmful gases. And what's more you're breathing them in right now! The shrinking scientists are checking out the 'air-raising truth...

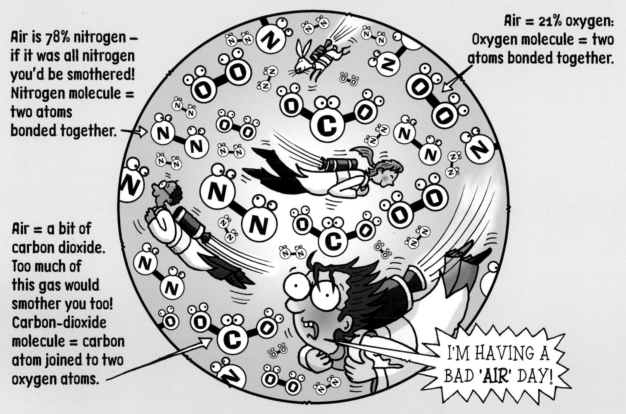

Air is 78% nitrogen – if it was all nitrogen you'd be smothered! Nitrogen molecule = two atoms bonded together.

Air = 21% oxygen: Oxygen molecule = two atoms bonded together.

Air = a bit of carbon dioxide. Too much of this gas would smother you too! Carbon-dioxide molecule = carbon atom joined to two oxygen atoms.

Those oxygen molecules are the only ones your body can use. They help your cells make energy and you can't live without them – which is why you breathe. Trouble is they're poisonous! Too much can damage your cells, which is why your body locks them up in haemoglobin. All in all, the air in your living room is pretty dangerous stuff.

Six sickening things you never knew you were breathing in

1 Fart molecules. Farts contain poisonous gases! There's methane (the gas people cook with) and hydrogen sulphide (the gas that smells of rotten eggs). The stinkiest molecules are indole and skatole made by gut bacteria.

2 Tiny flakes of dead skin, dead dust mites and oodles of microscopic mite poo.

3 Dried snot. One second after you sneeze, snotty droplets dry into crusty microscopic lumps. Just imagine alien micro-spacecraft packed with viruses. You breathe them in or they land on your hands. Then they explore your nostrils next time you pick your nose.

4 Pollen. Plants make pollen in flowers and pass it on in order to make seeds, but a lot of humans are allergic to pollen. They treat pollen like a germ with sneezing and extra snot. What a treat!

5 Fungal spores. Fungi include moulds and spores are like microscopic seeds. Each fungus makes billions of spores. Each spore can live 40 years and it can blow on the wind for thousands of kilometres. No wonder your bread goes mouldy! (See page 66 for more foul fungal facts.)

6 Cat spit. When your cat licks herself her tongue flicks spit. One quarter of a teaspoonful of spit floats about until it plops on your pizza. That's how the Tiddles slobbers on your supper...

BET YOU NEVER KNEW!

You breathe 15,000 litres of air in a year. You can check how clean it is by inspecting your earwax. In a dirty city your earwax could be dark brown from pollution.

SPIT AND SNOT

Can you spot the spit and snot on your living-room floor? Well, there are tiny traces of spit and snot everywhere – even on this page!

SNOT! ---- YES IT SNIS!

In fact there's more to snot than drippy noses and embarrassing bogeys. Snot traps dirt and bacteria. Tiny hairs in your nose waft the revolting gunk towards your throat. Then you swallow it. Yummm! Mind you, there is an even more revolting way to get snot in your mouth...

Could you be a snot scientist?

Indian boffins Chittaranjan Andrade and BS Srihari asked teenagers about nose picking. What did they find?

a) Half the teenagers picked their noses and some made snot sandwiches to share with their special friends.

b) All the teenagers picked their noses and 7% did it TWENTY times a day.

MMM, TASTY FILLING...

PICKED IT MYSELF!

Answer:

b) What's more 4.5% admitted picnicking on the putrid pickings (and I bet lots more did it in secret). In 1966 US scientist Sidney Tarachow studied bogey-munchers. The stupid snot-snackers claimed their snot was tasty. This is odd because it's oozing with dirt and germs.

Boost your word power with Horrible Science!

Here are some posh medical words for anyone with a nose for science...

Vibrissae (vi-bris-say) = nose hairs that guard against dirt and flies. Elderly male teachers have extra-long vibrissae.

Rhinorrhea (rhino-rear) = yellow or green runny snot oozing from your nose. The Author had this problem in the last chapter.

GRNNN!

SHNUFFLE!

Rhinotillexomania (rhino-till-exo-may-ne-a) = picking your nose.

18

Hmm – let's talk about something more tasteful. What about spit? Spit moistens your food and helps it go down. You may like to know that spit contains mucin – the protein found in snot. That's what makes spit so delightfully gloopy. So what else do you know about this vital fluid?

The load of dribble quiz

Don't sit there dribbling – answer TRUE or FALSE!

1 Spit can be used to clean valuable old paintings.

2 It's a good idea to lick your wounds.

3 One ml of spit contains 80 human cells.

4 Sometimes one of the tubes feeding spit into a person's mouth gets blocked. It can unblock suddenly and shoot a jet of spit from their mouth without warning.

Answers:

1 True – one moist cotton bud and your priceless old master is a lot cleaner.

2 False - spit can clean wounds in an emergency but it's best to use clean water.

3 False – it's eight million. Not to mention 500 million bacteria.

4 True – if this happened to you, you might get told off for spitting!

BET YOU NEVER KNEW!

When people used to chew tobacco they spat vile brown gobs of tobacco and brown spit. So they spat into a container called a spittoon. When one US baseball star spat in the umpire's face his fans gave him a special present. It was a giant spittoon overflowing with foamy gobby-drool.

DISGUSTING DUST

Is there dust in the living room? Let's take a closer look. You may see a few things that you wish you hadn't seen…

Flake of human skin — every minute you shed 40,000 flakes of flaky dead skin. That's over 1 g per day. Keep it and by the end of a year you'll have 0.4 kg of mouldy rotten flesh. What a lovely New Year present for someone you don't like!

Cat hair (see page 32).

Tiny bit of grit 1/33 mm across. Someone brought it in on their shoes when they forgot to wipe their feet. The grit came from a distant desert and blew in on the wind.

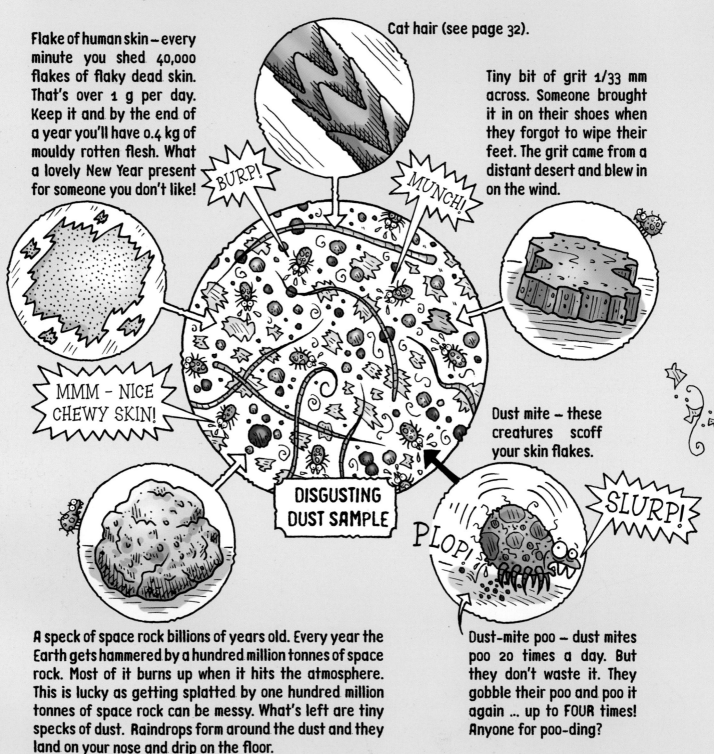

MMM – NICE CHEWY SKIN!

BURP!

MUNCH!

DISGUSTING DUST SAMPLE

Dust mite — these creatures scoff your skin flakes.

PLOP!

SLURP!

A speck of space rock billions of years old. Every year the Earth gets hammered by a hundred million tonnes of space rock. Most of it burns up when it hits the atmosphere. This is lucky as getting splatted by one hundred million tonnes of space rock can be messy. What's left are tiny specks of dust. Raindrops form around the dust and they land on your nose and drip on the floor.

Dust-mite poo — dust mites poo 20 times a day. But they don't waste it. They gobble their poo and poo it again … up to FOUR times! Anyone for poo-ding?

In 1983 a scientific survey found that dust is oozing with fibres from clothing, grease, plaster, human and animal hair. House dust isn't stuff you want to share a house with!

Vacuum cleaner to the rescue?

'MUM!' I hear you yell. 'Pleeease hoover up this disgusting dust!' It's a good idea – but most vacuum cleaners don't suck up everything. We asked the shrinking scientists to hoover the Baron's living room…

COUGH!

SPLUTTER!

CHOKE!

Dust mites cling to carpet – some manage to hang on.

Mite poo sucks through vacuum cleaner filter and sprays over scientists.

YEESH!

UGHHH!

Cleaner pushes air out of the way.

Air and dust drawn in behind the cleaner – this dust isn't sucked up.

THEY SHOULD HAVE READ THIS PAGE FIRST!

HOUSE OF HORRORS

Disgusting dust mite challenge

This book is jumping with disgusting dust mites. How many dust mites can you count? Answer on page 77!

CHOMP! NIBBLE! MUNCH! HI! G-DOING!

WHAT'S SQUIRMING ON YOUR SKIN?

Why bother with skin? After all, it messes up your home and ends up in a dust mite's dinner! Let's hear what Dr Grimgrave, the world's most dismal doctor, has to say...

WITHOUT SKIN YOU'D BE DEAD!

TELL ME ABOUT IT!

Dr G says that the flaky bits on your carpet are just the outermost scuffed-off layer* of your complex body covering. In fact your skin cells take two months to get to the surface. Then they die and flake off. If they didn't die you'd have to shed your skin, like an insect, before you could grow.

*Scientists call it the epidermis (ep-pee-der-mis).

Here are a few other interesting things that drop off your skin. Have you seen them in your home?

COSY AND WARM **AND** IT SMELLS OF CHEESE... PERFECT!

1 Sweat droplets. You've got two million sweat glands. No wonder some people drip on the carpet or leave sweaty footprints on the bathroom floor! Sweat evaporates from warm skin and takes away heat. Each of your feet loses 118 ml of sweat daily. The sweat soaks into your socks and gets mixed with dead skin. Bacteria guzzle the goo and puff out cheesy whiffs.

GOBBLE! MUNCH! CHOMP!

2 Hair. Hair is made of a protein called keratin. Each hair grows from a tiny pit called a follicle with its own tiny blood vessel. Here's something to think about next time one of your mum's hairs turns up in your soup. At least it's not one of your dad's armpit hairs. They often have bacteria glued to them like globby baubles. The mangy microbes gobble fats from armpit oil glands.

3 Fingernails (and toenails). Hopefully there aren't any toenails in your soup. They're made of keratin too. Nails have the job of protecting your fingers and toes. And nails stop them getting squished flat when you press on them.

NICE THUMBNAIL!

HMM, LET'S TEST IT...

Dare you discover ... how to test your health using your fingernails?

You will need:

Your fingernails (so stop chewing them NOW!)

What you do:

Press one of your nails with a finger. You will need to press firmly.

You should find:

The nail turns pale. The pink colour returns in a second or two. The pink colour comes from tiny blood vessels under the nail. When people lose a lot of blood the colour is slower to come back. This is a test that doctors often do in an emergency.

PRESS!

YOU'LL LIVE!

BET YOU NEVER KNEW!

1 It's possible to make human skin into a drum. Dying Czech hero Jan Zizka (1360–1424) wanted his skin to be made into a drum and beaten when his homeland was in danger. I guess a hero like Jan took a lot of beating...

2 One man has BLUE skin! In the 1990s an American man rubbed his dry skin with a silver remedy. It worked but his skin changed colour. The Baron decided to try this treatment on Monster Boy.

I'M FEELING BLUE!

YOU'RE IN THE PINK OF HEALTH!

CELL SECRETS

Let's take a closer look at those scabby skin flakes in your home. You'll see they're made of cells. Cells are horribly interesting…

Did you know…?

Your longest cells are nerve cells that carry signals to and from your brain. These stringy monsters can be one metre long.

Your longest-lived cells include brain cells. They can live for 100 years.

Your shortest-lived cells are lining your mouth and guts. They're replaced every five days.

Could you be a cell genius?

Simply match the descriptions to the cells!

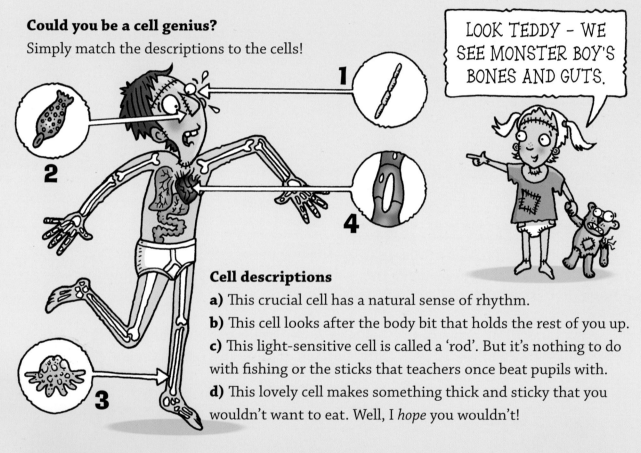

LOOK TEDDY – WE SEE MONSTER BOY'S BONES AND GUTS.

Cell descriptions

a) This crucial cell has a natural sense of rhythm.

b) This cell looks after the body bit that holds the rest of you up.

c) This light-sensitive cell is called a 'rod'. But it's nothing to do with fishing or the sticks that teachers once beat pupils with.

d) This lovely cell makes something thick and sticky that you wouldn't want to eat. Well, I *hope* you wouldn't!

Answers:

1c) It's in your eye – so it's something to do with pupils after all!

2d) It's a goblet cell and makes snot. They're found in your mouth, guts and lungs too.

3b) It's an osteoblast (os-tee-oh-blast) and it builds bones. Your bones are mainly mineral crystals but building them is a never-ending job. (It's probably done by a skeleton staff.)

4a) It's a cell of your cardiac muscle that squeezes according to an electrical rhythm produced by other cells. If it didn't your heart wouldn't beat and you'd be dead-beat.

Cells sound awesome don't they? But the thing that sends scientists reeling to the ceiling is what's inside that weird wall. Each one of your skin cells and most of your body cells is like a scary alien space base full of robots...

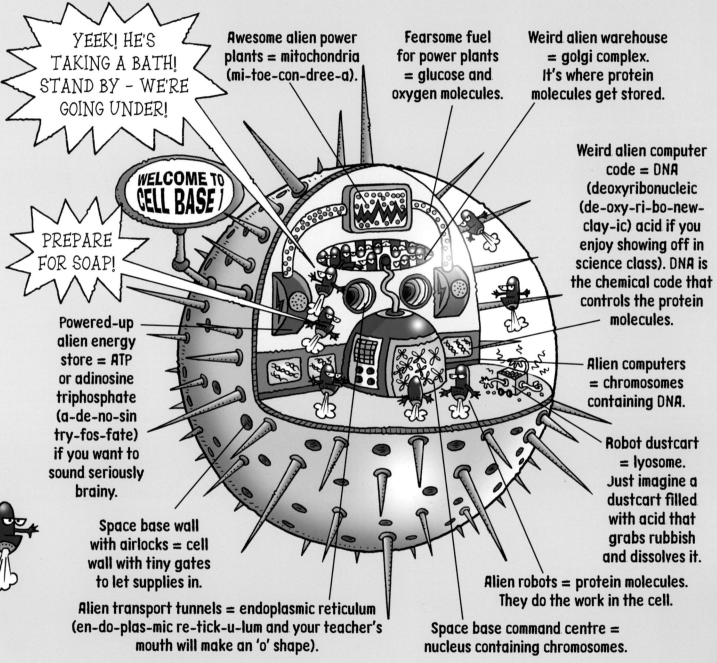

YEEK! HE'S TAKING A BATH! STAND BY - WE'RE GOING UNDER!

PREPARE FOR SOAP!

WELCOME TO CELL BASE!

Awesome alien power plants = mitochondria (mi-toe-con-dree-a).

Fearsome fuel for power plants = glucose and oxygen molecules.

Weird alien warehouse = golgi complex. It's where protein molecules get stored.

Weird alien computer code = DNA (deoxyribonucleic (de-oxy-ri-bo-new-clay-ic) acid if you enjoy showing off in science class). DNA is the chemical code that controls the protein molecules.

Powered-up alien energy store = ATP or adinosine triphosphate (a-de-no-sin try-fos-fate) if you want to sound seriously brainy.

Alien computers = chromosomes containing DNA.

Robot dustcart = lyosome. Just imagine a dustcart filled with acid that grabs rubbish and dissolves it.

Space base wall with airlocks = cell wall with tiny gates to let supplies in.

Alien robots = protein molecules. They do the work in the cell.

Alien transport tunnels = endoplasmic reticulum (en-do-plas-mic re-tick-u-lum and your teacher's mouth will make an 'o' shape).

Space base command centre = nucleus containing chromosomes.

Incredible – eh? And what a waste to leave millions of them on the floor to feed the dust mites! But it gets even more eye-popping! When the body needs another cell, the cell divides. It can even copy its DNA. How many spacecraft can copy themselves?

SQUISHY SKIN DISEASES

Scrabble about on your living-room carpet and you could find real horrors. I mean the nasty things that fall off your skin when things go wrong. Fancy finding a crusty dried-up scab or a nice blob of dried-up pus?

The shrinking scientists have found some scabby scraps of diseased skin on the Baron's carpet. Sorry about the pus on these pages!

1 Dandruff makes your skin flake in odious oily lumps. It goes really well with your best black top. Some people get dandruff on their eyebrows.

FASCINATING DANDRUFF, DON'T YOU THINK?

SNOW!

2 Eczema is dry, red, raised skin with lovely oozing, crusty blisters. It's caused by an allergy. Eczema runs in families. I bet the pus runs in families too.

3 Chicken-pox blisters are filled with foul fluid and the vicious chicken-pox virus. Measles blisters are similar. You get blisters when your skin is rubbed – for example, by tight trainers. This makes your blood vessels leak fluid.

4 Psoriasis (sore-ri-asis) is when skin cells form too quickly. Itchy slabs of scaly skin develop at the joints and sometimes cover the body. The poor victim looks more scary than Monster Boy.

5 Impetigo starts off as a blob of blisters. They get worse and crusty as bacteria spread under the skin. They often appear around the mouth. At least your granny won't want a kiss!

26

6 Warts – a virus fools your skin into making a lump of extra cells. Some doctors treat warts with liquid nitrogen. The warts freeze in seconds and drop off later.

7 Hives are nothing to do with bees. People get them when blood vessels widen due to inflammation.

8 Monster Boy's got spots. They form when your skin makes too much oil. Oil, dead skin and bacteria block a sweat gland. It swells. Your body orders white blood cells to battle the bacteria. That disgusting pus is dead white blood cells and bacteria.

DON'T SQUEEZE IT! YOU'LL LET GERMS UNDER YOUR SKIN... YOU'LL MAKE IT WORSE! OH YUCK... TOO LATE!

Could you be a spot spotter?

Simply match the spot to its scientific name…

Scientific name	Description
1 Macule	**a)** Round raised splotch
2 Papule	**b)** Bigger blister than 3
3 Nodule	**c)** Flat splotch
4 Plaque	**d)** Bigger spot than 2
5 Bulla	**e)** Flat area more raised-up than 1.

Answers:

1c, **2a**, **3d**, **4e**, **5b** But it's nothing to do with bulls, bull-eyes, eyeballs or footballs.
Spots sound seriously sickening but the next chapter is even sicker! Guess what – your pet's pests could turn your home into a scary safari…

LICE, FLEAS AND PESKY PETS

Have you got a pet at home? Well, they do say that with a pet you're never alone. And it's true! Some pets have lice, some have fleas so there's quite a crowd…

ARRRRRRRRRGH!

What's that scream? Oh dear – the Baron's spotted a head louse on his wig!

We'll start with…

(NOT) WANTED DEAD OR ALIVE!

For Crimes Against Humanity
THE LOATHSOME LICE GANG

THE HEAD LOUSE

A master of disguise, the head louse can change colour to match your hair.

Blonde   Brunette

Ginger   Grey

Three sinister species. Known aliases – the Body, Pubic and Head Louse

Pincers for grabbing hair

Mouthparts for sucking blood

Everything you ever wanted to ask your teacher about lice but were too scared to ask

1 Most animals have their very own louse species (as you've just found out, we have three). Lucky lice-free creatures include whales, armadillos and the duck-billed platypus.

2 Body lice don't live on bodies. They hide in our clothes and jump on us when they get peckish. Their favourite bite sites are bums and tums. Every three to six hours they jab their mouthparts into our flesh. Their mouthparts are like two drinking straws. One straw slices a blood vessel and the other straw injects spit with an anti-blood-clotting substance. Lice like clean people but they're not fussy. Oh yes – and they love a crunchy dead skin snack.

3 Head lice are a horror in the home. All clothes and bedding must be washed. Lice mums glue up to 300 eggs to your hairs. (They can glue themselves by mistake but who cares about them?) You need special shampoo to zap the lice and a fine comb to remove the eggs (they're called nits).

4 Teachers get head lice too.
Do head teachers get head teacher head lice?

Mind you, lice don't have it all their own way. They die out if the animal they live on becomes rare. This happened to the passenger pigeon louse and could happen to the pygmy hog lurking louse (and no, I am not making these names up). It's a lousy way to go!

Ooops – sorry! I've just remembered that this chapter is supposed to be about pets! Well, it's true that pet dogs can carry dog lice. A dog louse looks like this…

Your dog might be upset to read that there are dog-biting and dog-sucking lice. The biting blighters dine on your dog's skin and the sinister suckers slurp blood! Luckily dog lice are quite rare.

BET YOU NEVER KNEW!
Some potty people keep lice as pets! In 1915 a scientist at the Lister Institute in Hertfordshire, England fed his pet parasite on his own blood. In 2008 seven Berlin artists staged an unusual art exhibition. They wore shower caps to stop their head lice escaping. The lice were part of the show.

FOUL FLEAS

If you've got a cat, there could be cat fleas hopping in your home. The shrinking scientists have caught one for us to look at – it's definitely up to scratch!

Narrow body ideal for slipping through hair

Bristles tangle in hair and make flea tricky to remove

Flea spit contains a substance that stops blood from clotting

SLOOOOOOP!

Pointy head for burrowing in Tiddles' flesh and sucking blood

Mouthparts like a straw for sucking blood

Here's a cat flea bedtime story to get you hopping into bed. And, what's more, it's true!

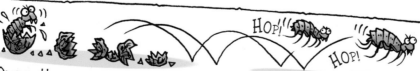

CRUNCH!

SUCK! SLURP!

Once upon a time a mummy and a daddy flea had lots of baby larvae. The larvae hatched from eggs and snuggled in the warm, cosy cat's bed. The poor little larvae were hungry.

But then the mummy and daddy flea and all the uncle and aunt fleas sucked blood from the cat.

PLOP!

CHOMP! MUNCH!

And they made lots of lovely blood-rich poo for the babies to eat.

The babies dined on dung until they turned into pupae.

HOP! HOP!

EEK!

Once they were grown-up they hopped off to seek their fortunes on the cat. And they all bit happily ever after!

Three foul flea facts (try saying that three times with a mouthful of fleas!)

1 There are more than 1,600 flea species. Each type of fussy flea prefers their favourite animal victim. That's why cat fleas rarely bite humans. We'd be hopping mad if they did!

2 A flea can jump 20 cm in the air and land 33 cm away. If a mad scientist turned you into a human-sized flea you'd have superhuman powers. You could leap a 90-metre office block and land 160 metres away. And do it hundreds of times a day.

IT'S FLEA BOY!

G-DOING!

3 Human fleas are rare because we're so clean. Well, most of us are!
Two hundred years ago, never mind cat fleas – *human* fleas were the problem. People were scratching their heads (and everywhere else) to get rid of them. One stupid solution was to cover your floor with cow poo. Another was to wear a trap round your neck...

Dare you discover ... how to make an eighteenth-century flea trap?

You will need:
A small pasta tube (macaroni is ideal)
Runny syrup
Teaspoon
30-cm length of thread

SYRUP

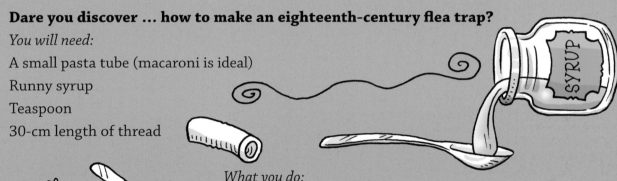

TASTY!

What you do:

1 Here's the tricky bit. Use the spoon to trickle a thin dribble of syrup into the tube. Do this over a sink. Some syrup might trickle into your mouth by mistake. Tell your mum that this is a vital stage in the experiment. She *might* fall for it!

2 Still with me? Great – now push the thread through the pasta tube and tie the ends together.

3 Hang your flea trap around your neck. The fleas will get stuck in the sticky syrup.
What's that? You don't have fleas? No problem – try it out on your flea-bitten cat!

PESKY PET PRESENTS
– part one

Pets are naturally messy creatures. I bet your pet has left a few of these putrid presents in your home …

Cat and dog hair. Cat and dog hair is just like ours. It's made of keratin and grows from pits in the skin. Trouble is your pet's hair gets everywhere. You'll find loads wherever they've been sleeping. And on your mum's best cushions. And on the spare bed just when the posh guests turn up.

Muddy paw prints. You know when Tiddles leaves muddy paw marks on the newly polished floor? Look closely and you'll see that on each side the front and rear paw marks are nearly in the same place. That's how cats walk.

Cat scent molecules. You can't see them, you can't smell them – but cats can. Glands on Tiddles' head make a scent substance. And she rubs her head on things like your trouser legs to spread the scent. The scent means – this is MINE! Your cat reckons she owns your trousers.

Slobbery doggie-dribble. Doggie-breath can be due to kidney or gum disease. Or maybe the miserable mutt has been munching raw meat or poo. I bet their drool is dripping with bacteria! Fancy a face-lick?

Sweaty paw prints. It's rotten being a cooked cat or a hot dog! Imagine having to wear a fur coat all summer. No wonder cool cats chill in the shade and hot hounds need plenty of water! Dogs cool down by panting. This takes heat from their hot bodies. Hot cats sweat between their toes. Look out for wet paw prints on a dry floor.

Chewed up doggie toys. Puppies love to chew. It relaxes them and stops the itching when their teeth are coming through. No wonder they chew toys and your dad's slippers end up soggy! Did you know one British springer spaniel scoffed 40 pairs of pants, 300 socks and the keys to his owner's car? Not all at once, I hasten to add...

GIMMEE THOSE CAR KEYS!

SCREEEEEEEK!

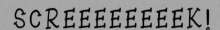

Scratched sofa. Tiddles scratches trees to sharpen her claws. She also spreads kitty scent and stretches her muscles. If there isn't a tree in your living room she'll be quite happy with the new sofa. Or your dad's trouser legs.

Dead mouse. It's a present. Tiddles thought you looked peckish. Try to look grateful!

DEAD MOUSE PONG!

RUMMAGE!

CAT EAR MITE

CAT EAR WAX

Cat ear mites. Imagine dust mites in your ear. Not nice – huh? Well, luckily we don't get them but some cats do. They make Tiddles' ears sore and gobble kitty earwax.

WORRY!

CRUNCH! CHEW! SUCK! NIBBLE! MUNCH! SCOFF!

Could you be an ear-mite scientist?
You are New York vet Robert Lopez. You wonder if cat ear mites can live in human ears. So you put mites in your ear. Soon you're in pain with parasites parading on your face every night. What do you do?

a) Stuff the mites back in the cat's ears.

b) Repeat the experiment ... TWICE!

Answer:

b) Robert was rewarded in 1994 with an IgNobel Prize for strange science. Another award went to the scientists who studied nose-picking.

PESKY PET PRESENTS
– part two

Not every home has a cat or a dog. Some people have pet birds instead...

Parrots are brainy birds. Before he hopped the perch in 2007, Alex the African Grey Parrot could count and tell his owner off for using the wrong word. Is your little brother this intelligent? Mind you it's not all feathered fun for parrots. Some have pesky parasites. Foul feather mites burrow in their skin. Feather lice chew their plumage. It's enough to make a bird sick as a parrot! Mind you, feathers are fascinating ... did you know that they're made of keratin like your nails?

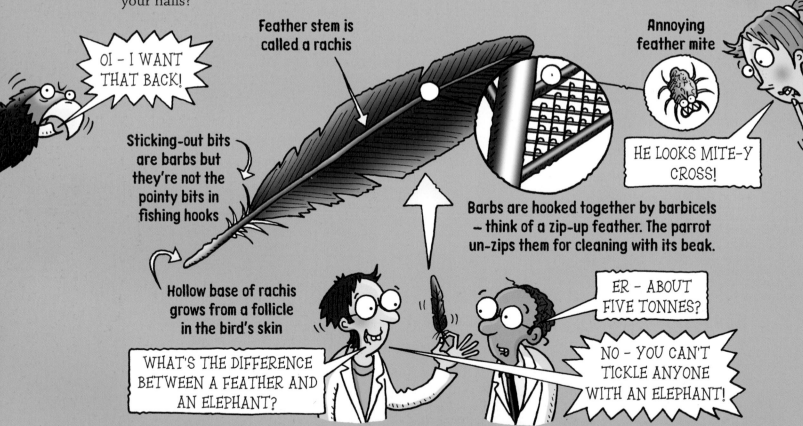

Mind you, it doesn't matter whether your pet is a dog, cat, parrot or peckish piranha fish. They all produce poo and sometimes do it in the wrong place…

Putrid pet poo facts

1 You might think your cat buries her poo. But cats also leave poo unburied to mark the edge of their territory. The nasty neighbour's cat leaves poo in your garden to tell your cat that she owns it. Dogs, guinea pigs and other beasts also use poo as a marker. Fortunately we don't.

2 Like human poo, pet poo is oozing with bacteria. There's a putrid protist parasite in cat poo called toxoplasma (tock-so-plas-ma). It lives in rat brains and makes the rat take silly risks. Eventualy the reckless rat gets chomped by a cat. And that's the putrid parasite's plan. It lives in cat guts too!

3 If you're a dog owner it's good manners to pick up your pet's poo. Not your idea of fun? No worries! A German inventor made a machine to suck the poo out of Fido before it plops on the pavement. I could tell you the details – but they're too disgusting!

4 Rabbits and guinea pigs gobble poo to digest the tough plant cells. This is called coprophagy (cop-pro-faggy) – which is Greek for 'poo-eating'. Rabbits relish squishy poo but they're not too keen on the hard, crusty stuff. How fussy can you get? Can you imagine what it would be like if humans did this? Going to a posh restaurant just wouldn't be the same!

BET YOU NEVER KNEW!
In 2007 a US pooch named Pepper ate $1000 in cash. You'll be delighted to read that Pepper's owners found $647 in Pepper's poo. So they took it to the bank to swap for nice clean cash.

WHAT'S HIDING IN YOUR HOME?

Your revolting residence might be home to more creatures than you know...
How many can you spot in the Baron's Castle?

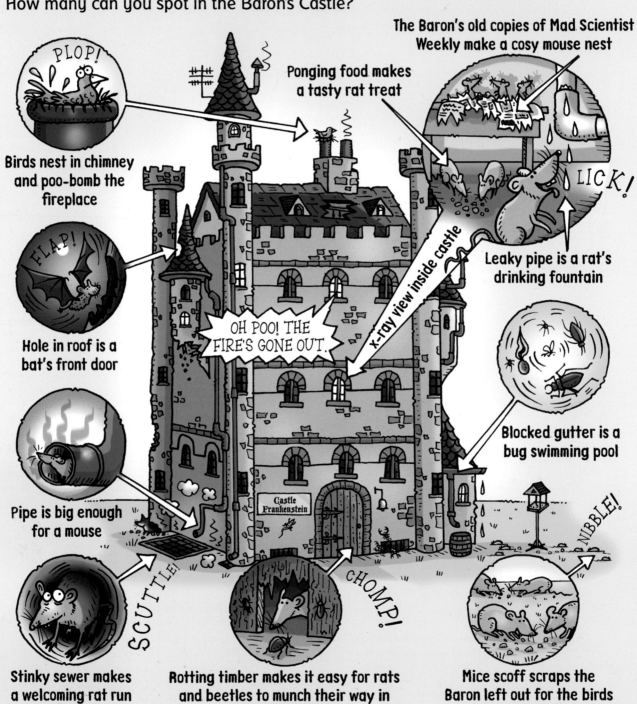

36

Did you spot all these creatures?

1 Foxes burrow under houses. Sounds fun? Monster Boy wasn't best pleased when a fox pooed in his smelly trainers. And he didn't enjoy being kept awake by screaming cubs.

2 Some bat species live in homes. They'll fill your attic with bat poo. When they die. they don't fall on the floor. Their claws lock in place. So they just hang there looking gruesome.

3 This cute little gecko lives in warm climates all over the world. Fancy a pet gecko? You can watch it climb all over your walls, catch bugs and even lick its eyeballs with its tongue.

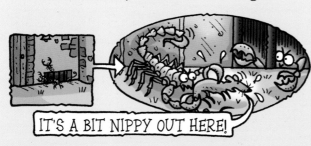

4 The Baron's dungeons are crawling with deadly scorpions. You only have to worry about them if you're in a hot country. There are about 1,500 species, but only about 25 harm humans.

Three reasons why having unwanted animals in your home is a good idea

1 If you ran out of food you could eat your unwanted animals. At the Nanjing food festival in China people snack on tasty skewered scorpions and centipedes.

2 If scorpions aren't your dish of the day you could try bats. How about a traditional Chinese boiled bat or a scrumptious Samoan fried bat? And you could invite the false vampire bat to dinner. It eats other bats and always chews them well to savour that unique batty flavour.

3 Be grateful that your scorpions, bats and gecko are getting rid of your unwanted bugs. In fact a bat scrunches 600 mosquitoes an hour. You could let your pet snake eat your rats and mice. Trouble is it might scoff the cat too!

BURGLAR BUGS

Just imagine you made a living creeping into people's houses and trashing them! That's what some bugs do. Hopefully your home isn't crawling with these little horrors!

CLEANING SERVICES

DOES YOUR HOSPITAL NEED A SPRING CLEAN? Pharaoh Ant Cleaning Services will eat your unwanted bloody bandages. We'll even leave a free sample of 19 disease-causing microbes to share with your patients!

UGH! I CAN'T EAT ANY MORE!

PHAROAH-NUFF!

Tired of your old home?

Carpenter Ant Services will get rid of it fast! We'll eat all those ugly old beams holding up your home.

CRUMPH!

NICE ONE!

If your house gets you down we'll bring it down!

MAKE GREASY STAINS A THING OF THE PAST!

The Grease Ants will remove all your grease and any dead rats or mice lying around! It's a free service! Don't be shy - apply today!

ARE PESTS SPOILING YOUR LIFE?

Call in Army Ant Pest Control (South America only). All two million of us will march through your living room and eat everything alive! Just make sure you wake granny up and put the cat out!

TOO LATE!

Tired of your damp kitchen?

Time to redecorate with Slug Services! We'll transform your boring old lino with beautiful silvery slime trails! All we ask are a few mouldy lettuce leaves the rabbit didn't want!

BUT I DID WANT THEM!

Old woodwork can be a worry!

You need Termite Timber Treatment! We'll eat your problem timber. And we'll even eat your non-problem timber! We'll chew through concrete if we have to. Then we'll build a GIGANTIC luxury termite nest where your home used to be!

Luxury air conditioning caused by rising warm air

CHOMP!

NEST FOR SALE

FEELING LONELY?

You need a pet house cricket! No kennel required – a pile of rotting rubbish will do! Your little pal will keep you company with its cheeky chirping. And it won't stop when you're trying to sleep.

CHIRRRRRRUP!

SHUT UP!

KIND-HEARTED FAMILY NEEDED!

It's a cold night. Could you offer a home to a poor little woodlouse family? Simply water your carpet with a watering can or your guests will dry out in the night! PS Please scatter rotting vegetables around your house for them to eat.

MUNCH!

THANKS!

BET YOU NEVER KNEW!

Are your bug guests getting you down? Just hope they don't invite their rotten relatives!

1 Time for a midnight feast. You tiptoe to the fridge and ... SQUISH! Your toes squelch a cold, slimy SLUG! Oh well, at least it's not a ghost slug. This sinister slobbery slitherer lurks in Asian caves. It scoffs bat poo and sucks worms like spaghetti. Luckily it doesn't come into houses and it doesn't gobble toes.

2 Cymothoa (simo-tho-a) is rotten relative of the woodlouse. It sneaks into a mouth of an unlucky spotted rose snapper fish and feasts on the fishy tongue. Then it scoffs the snapper's supper.

YUM YUM!

GRRRRR!

NOT-SO-NICE MICE

Kids' cartoons make out that mice are nice. In fact they're as cute as a dose of flu! Well, you wouldn't want one in your home – that's all I can say! The shrinking scientists have found a mouse in the Baron's gruesome grandfather clock…

Manky mouse quiz

Are you a mouse mastermind? All the figures in these facts are bigger or smaller. But which are more and which are less?

1 Mice pee *all the time* and they use it to send chemical messages to other mice. A mouse can pee 50 litres of wee per year.

2 When they're not peeing, they're poo-ing. A mouse can plop 6 poo pellets a day.

3 The other thing mice do is breed. A pair of mice can produce 20 babies in one year.

4 The babies breed as soon as they can. So you could end up with 10,000 munching, peeing, poo-ing, breeding mice by the end of year!

Answers:

1 LESS. It's 7 and that's a lot if you're mouse-sized. In fact mice don't even drink – they get the moisture they need from food.

2 MORE. Believe or not the answer's 70. And they'll happily poo in your pants ... and your lunch! They're not exactly squeaky clean.

3 MORE – we're talking 160.

4 LESS– it's 1000 and that's enough! Oh well, it'll give the cat something to chase. When she can be bothered!

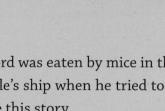

Using your lunch as a loo isn't too nice but mice have other horrible habits. Their front teeth don't stop growing and they gnaw to wear them down. If you had teeth like this you'd gnaw anything – including a school dinner. Either that or end up with teeth like a hippo! Mice gnaw through computer and TV cables but sadly teachers don't fall for the old 'mice ate my homework' excuse like they used to.

Three mouse facts to squeak to your friends about

1 According to writer Roger of Howden an evil German Lord was eaten by mice in the Middle Ages. The murderous mice even swam after the nasty noble's ship when he tried to get away. It wasn't a mice way to go. Mind you, experts don't believe this story.

2 In the eighteenth century foolish fashionable people shaved off their eyebrows. Instead they wore mouseskin eyebrows stuck on with smelly fish glue.

3 Some mice go surfing. In 2005 Australian Shane Willmott took three pet mice surfing on tiny boards. He even dyed their coats. That way he could find his squeaky pals when they fell in the sea.

HMM, THINK I'LL LEAVE THE TAILS OFF NEXT TIME.

41

ROTTEN RATS

Rats are rotten. In fact they're so rotten there isn't just one rotten rat species – there are two! They're really at home in a house of horror!

Can you spot EIGHT differences between them?

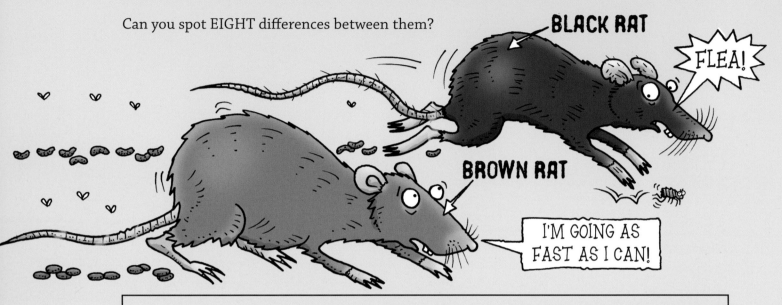

BLACK RAT

FLEA!

BROWN RAT

I'M GOING AS FAST AS I CAN!

5 Black rat has more hair on its ears.	
4 Black rat's nose is more pointed.	rat is flat-footed.
3 Brown rat is bigger.	**8** Black rat runs on its toes and brown
2 Black rat has a longer tail.	**7** Black rat's poo is slightly more curved.
1 The colour difference is a bit of a giveaway.	**6** Black rat is more slender.

How fascinating! Let's take a closer view of that brown rat...

Rat whiskers send nerve signals to the rat's brain as they bend. Rats with curly whiskers can't sense things so well.

AHHH!

SAY, "AHHH"

Rats can't see too well

Rat teeth darken as they grow older

Rat teeth enamel is harder than human teeth

You don't often see black and brown rats together. Black rats are rare. They like roofs – there are loads of black rats in the Baron's awful attic. Brown rats live in sewers and the Baron's dreadful dungeons. Of course rats aren't known for their good manners...

Humans have been trying to get rid of rats for as long as rats have been trying to scoff our suppers. Here's my favourite rat-trap ever...

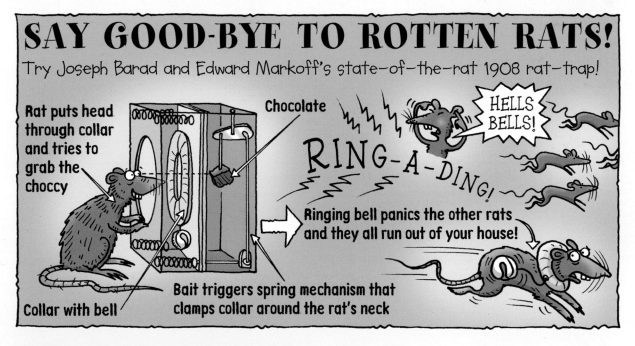

SAY GOOD-BYE TO ROTTEN RATS!

Try Joseph Barad and Edward Markoff's state-of-the-rat 1908 rat-trap!

Rat puts head through collar and tries to grab the choccy

Chocolate

HELLS BELLS!

RING-A-DING!

Ringing bell panics the other rats and they all run out of your house!

Collar with bell

Bait triggers spring mechanism that clamps collar around the rat's neck

Actually, it didn't work. Oh well, if rats eat your supper – why not eat the rats?

BET YOU NEVER KNEW!

In 1994, the Super Deer restaurant opened in Canton, China. It served rat recipes such as rat and rice, fried rat and juicy rat kebabs. The rat restaurant was an instant hit. It was less popular with the rats. They were boiled alive before being cooked.

WHAT'S CRAWLING IN YOUR KITCHEN?

What's your kitchen like? Is it clean enough to eat your dinner off the floor? Or dirty enough to have last night's dinner on the floor? Well, I hope it's not as bad as the Baron's kitchen!

Bacteriological analysis of Baron Frankenstein's kitchen

by the Shrinking Scientists

We detected billions of bacteria on the food preparation areas and chopping board. There are almost as many around the sink. The serving and cooking areas aren't so bad. We think this is because most of the bacteria get cooked. Junior nearly got cooked too when he got trapped in the cooker but we've put the flames out now.

1 Bacteria hide in the greasy dust behind the food blender.

2 Cupboard full of rotting food.

3 In the whole history of the world, the microwave hasn't been cleaned once!

4 The bin is in a warm damp place where bacteria like to breed. It hasn't been emptied for a *very* long while…

5 Uggh! Cockroach snacking on rotting cat food.

6 Fruit flies exploring rotting fruit.

7 Bloodstained chopper and board are dripping with bacteria.

8 Mouse poo on floor.

9 Little Monster's been dropping crumbs and slopping spills on the floor. Pity no-one's wiped them up.

10 Last night's supper left on table. This is great news for the fly and a free drop-in fast food stop for hungry airborne bacteria.

11 Smelly dishcloth is a putrid paradise for microbes.

12 UGGGH! Green fungus on dishes! Looks like someone hasn't been washing up lately!

13 Dried fruit soaking moisture and mould spores from the air.

14 Tea towel is a happy home for microbes.

15 Leaving fridge door open allows it to warm up so bacteria can multiply faster.

16 Cooker hood is stuffed with encrusted fat and condensation. It's a great hideout for bacteria.

In 2009 nearly one third of all the food bought in the USA was thrown away uneaten. In the UK people chucked out 6.7 million tonnes of food including 359,000 tonnes of potatoes and 160,000 tonnes of meat and fish. But of course the food wasn't wasted. It fed billions of bacteria, and millions of mice and rats. Oh yes, and fruit flies.

BET YOU NEVER KNEW!
Scientists made a fruit fly … drive a car. OK, it was only a toy car. In 2008 Swiss scientists linked a fruit fly's flight in a virtual reality chamber to a toy car. The fly's movements steered the car.

HOW TO YOU MAKE A FRUIT FLY?

YOU THROW IT AT MR FLUFFY!

CLONK!

OW!

MANKY MEAL MICROBES

So you thought the Baron's kitchen was bad? Chances are that your kitchen is squirming with bacteria too! After all it's a free hotel with free food – what more does a bacterium want? Randall Scandall asked a bacterium to come clean. But bacteria don't come clean – they come dirty!

The Horrible Science Interview
with Randall Scandal

RS: I'm in Baron Frankenstein's fridge talking to a bacterium. What's it like being a microbe?

B: It's tough, man! Last night I was stuck at the wrong end of the supper table. Good thing I can swim faster for my size than your Olympic swimming stars!

RS: So you made it in time for dinner?

B: Yeah – the Baron gave me a lift in the dishcloth. It picked me up like a giant flying saucer. It's warm and cosy with lots of food. It's almost as nice as the toilet! Trouble is, I fell off!

RS: What happened?

B: I floated onto Monster Boy's dinner. It was delicious! More microbe mates joined me and we started dividing and multiplying our numbers.

RS: Hey I didn't know bacteria did maths!

B: Ha ha – that's nearly funny! Soon there were billions of us. Then that beastly Baron stuck us in the fridge. IT'S COLD IN HERE! We need a warm place like Monster Boy's guts! Or how about yours?

There are lots of bacteria you wouldn't want to share your supper with. They're in Dr Grimgrave's latest book. It's not on sale at all good bookshops because it's much too boring!

MY FAVOURITE DISEASES

BY DR H GRIMGRAVE

Chapter 7

HARMFUL INTESTINAL BACTERIA 1 HAVE KNOWN

My idiot patients are always wasting my time with food-poisoning problems. If only they stored their food properly by keeping it covered, I would have more time for important medical research. What these brainless buffoons ought to realize is that food needs to be cooked all the way through to kill harmful bacteria.

Of course, harmful gut microbes have a certain fascination. They multiply and produce poisons that trigger vomiting and diarrhoea. My idiot patients pass on the bacteria in diarrhoea by not washing their hands after visiting the toilet. Disgusting!

EXAMPLES OF FASCINATING BACTERIA

Listeria — live in soil and rotting materials. They get onto food from dirty hands and live in fridges. They cause aches and fever for days and the idiot comes bleating to me about flu!

Vibrio — these bacteria are especially fond of seafood. Within 24 hours they cause violent vomiting and stomach cramps. These microbes are totally shellfish, ha ha!

Bacilli — a large group of bacteria. They are common in cooked rice. This is why only idiots keen on regurgitation* should re-heat rice once it has cooled in a fridge.

*Doctor-speak for vomiting

Feeling depressed? Dr Grimgrave has this effect on people! Oh well – cheer up! These gruesome germs probably don't live in your fridge. And your food is ready to fight back!

FREAKY FOOD FIGHTBACK

Picture this – you're about to snack on a yummy yolky egg. Then the egg eats you! That's what happens to bacteria. There are lots of foods that give bacteria a bad time. How many have you got at home?

As long as your cereal stays in an airtight container, your breakfast is safe. Like you, bacteria need moisture. Dried foods like biscuits, crisps, dried pasta, coffee and tea are no good for them.

...BUT WE DON'T HAVE A TIN OPENER!

Cheese is set with the aid of friendly bacteria. These germ good guys make a substance that keeps other bacteria away. Trouble is, salmonella and other bad bacteria make your cheese slimy. And yeasts and fungi grow on the outside.

Sterilized milk is a bacterium's worst nightmare. The milk was heated to 112°C for 15 minutes. That's enough to kill all bacteria deader than the dinosaurs.

WE LOVE BAKED BEANS...

BACTERIA KEEP OUT!

Salty foods suck moisture from a bacterium until it shrivels up like a microbe mummy. This is called osmosis (os-mo-sis). Sugar has a similar effect. No wonder bacteria don't scoff sweets!

Bacteria make yogurt from milk. They add lactic acid, which makes milk too acidic for other bacteria. Fungi and yeasts still get in on the act.

Tinned foods are heated in the tin. Any bacteria that dare sneak inside get cooked and any bacteria outside can't get in.

WE NEED IT FOR THE NEXT PAGE...

I'VE CRACKED THE EGG!

YOU'LL HAVE TO SHELL OUT FOR A NEW ONE.

This egg is a deadly germ trap...

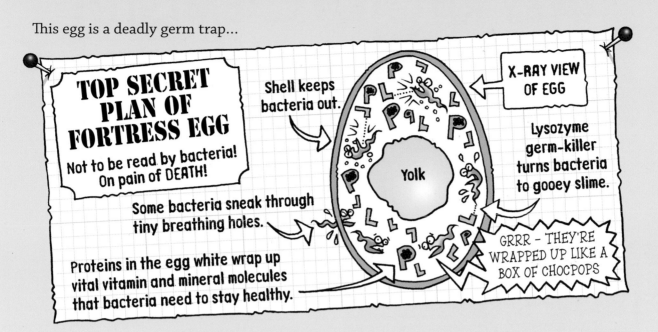

When bacteria win the battle they feed on your food with rotten results. The Baron's evil pal Count Vomito has made these foods into a spoilt supper. Fancy a nibble? Thought not!

Have you got any miserably mouldy food lurking at the back of your fridge...?

CRAZY KITCHEN CHEMISTRY

Wouldn't it be totally cool if your home had a mad science lab full of crazy chemicals? Well, it does – it's called 'the kitchen'! Here's what's in it…

Weird water

Water might seem a bit wet. After all what's the point of a drink you can't taste? But it's actually mad and crazy. Did you know…?
Water was first made in exploding stars.
Each water molecule contains three atoms.

The atoms share some electrons. The oxygen atom pulls nearby water molecules. This draws them together and makes water drippy. Like other substances, water can be a solid, liquid or gas depending on how hot it is…

HAVE A COCKROACH LOLLY!

Water below 0°C forms a solid.

COOL!

ANYONE FOR COCKROACH TEA?

Above 100°C, water forms a type of gas called a vapour.

ERK!

Instant Expert – crazy crystals
Lots of substances form crystals. Here are two from your kitchen…
1 Strange salt
Salt molecules are made of sodium and chlorine.

Sodium **Na – Cl** Chlorine

Greedy chlorine grabs an electron from sodium. The atoms get bonded together.

WE'RE STUCK!

Crystal

Salt molecules pack together to form square-ish crystals.

2 Sickly sugar
Sugar crystals are more complicated. Each sugar molecule contains a fructose and glucose molecule. They're bonded by another molecule…

WE'LL STICK TO OUR JOB!

molecule = one Hydrogen and one Oxygen

Salt and sugar crystals dissolve in water. Water molecules pull the salt and sugar molecules apart. Monster Boy has just performed this interesting experiment…

PFFFT - WHO PUT SALT IN MY TEA?

Your crazy kitchen lab has acids like lemon juice (citric acid) and vinegar (ethnoic acid). If you mix acid with water it produces protons. The protons make an electric force that rips other molecules to bits!

Dare you discover … how to make an acid drink?

You will need:

Lemon juice

2 tea bags

Measuring jug

2 glasses

Teaspoon and dessertspoon

A4 sheet of white paper

What you do:

1 Fill the jug with 200 ml hot water from the tap. Add the two tea bags and leave them to soak for one minute. Give the teabags a quick stir and squeeze with the teaspoon and then remove them from the jug. Pour 100 ml of tea into each glass.

2 Label the glasses A and B. Add one dessertspoon of lemon juice to A and stir well. Place them on the white paper to compare colours.

You should find:

Glass A has yellow tea and Glass B stays the same (it reminds you what colour the tea should be).

This is because:

Tea contains brown and yellow colours. Acid protons bond to molecules of brown colour and make it fade. You added citric acid protons to glass A. This faded the brown and left the yellow. Oh well, some people like lemon tea. And some people don't!

Cockroach from page 50

LEMON TEA IS BETTER FOR YOU… WELL, IT'S BETTER FOR ME!

Luckily, the acids in your crazy kitchen chemistry lab aren't strong enough to dissolve you. Otherwise a drop of lemon juice could turn you into lemon squash.

51

CREEPY COCKROACHES
AND OTHER PANTRY PESTS

It's not just barfing bacteria that hang out in your kitchen. There's a small army of pantry pests ready to bring terror to your teatime. I hope you don't get a visit from these guys…

The Horrible Science Interview
with Randall Scandal

I tracked down the American cockroach to a run-down diner.

RS: How does it feel to be Public Enemy Number One?

AC: Me and the boys ain't done no one any harm! Just ask my old mom – oh no, you can't cos I ate her.

RS: What about moving into our homes?

MUNCH! CHEW! CHOMP!

AC: Yeah, well, we do that. We like it warm and moist and it's not like we eat your food or nothing. OK so we do, but leave it around. That's an invitation in my neighbourhood. Anyhow, we pay for it…

RS: What do you mean?

AC: Like we leave poo and vomit and plenty bacteria. Some of them cause very unusual diseases. In fact the boys have just left some in your sandwiches as a goodwill gesture.

SPLURP!

BLEURGH!

RS: Thanks, guys! How big is the gang?

AC: Well, there's me, the German, the Asian and the oriental cockroach. We do all the household crime, but we've got 4,000 associate species, like the stinking cockroach. He sprays stink gas. Say, would ya like to meet him?

RS: No thanks!

AC: Gee – that's tough 'cos he wants to meet you!

YURGH! PFFFFFFFFT!

Want to see a cockroach up close and horrible? The shrinking scientists aren't scared!

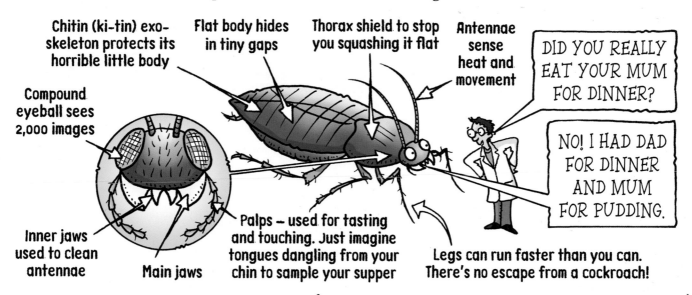

Chitin (ki-tin) exo-skeleton protects its horrible little body

Flat body hides in tiny gaps

Thorax shield to stop you squashing it flat

Antennae sense heat and movement

Compound eyeball sees 2,000 images

Inner jaws used to clean antennae

Main jaws

Palps – used for tasting and touching. Just imagine tongues dangling from your chin to sample your supper

Legs can run faster than you can. There's no escape from a cockroach!

DID YOU REALLY EAT YOUR MUM FOR DINNER?

NO! I HAD DAD FOR DINNER AND MUM FOR PUDDING.

BET YOU NEVER KNEW!

Cockroaches eat other cockroaches. They even lunch on their legs if they have to. They're so unfussy that they'll eat this book and relish the tasteless jokes!

Cruel cockroaches quiz

Which cockroach facts are just too creepy to be true?

1 If you've got a roach problem all you have to do is let giant centipedes roam your home.

2 An artist taught a cockroach to paint pictures.

3 An American man swallowed eleven hissing cockroaches in one mouthful.

Answers:

1 True – They love a crunchy cockroach snack. Now all you have to worry about is finding a giant centipede in your slipper.

2 False, sort of. The artist Steven Kutcher paints the insect's legs and lets it wander over his pictures.

3 False – Travis Fraser of Kentucky put the cockroaches in his mouth. But he let them go afterwards. They were his pets!

At least some people *like* cockroaches. I don't think anyone in the world likes the bug on the next page!

FILTHY FLIES

You can add horror to your home by inviting a filthy fly for dinner…

The shrinking scientists in… Fly or die!

NEARLY! Sorry readers, I'm trying to catch that annoying fly. WHACK – ooops I've splatted it! Oh well, let's take a look at the squished body bits…

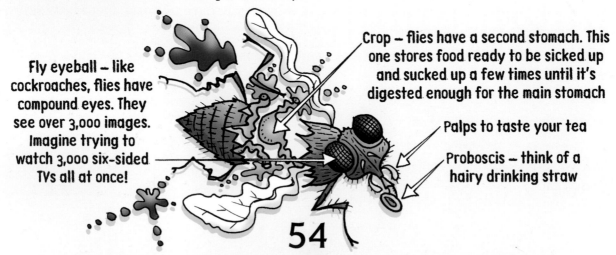

Fly eyeball – like cockroaches, flies have compound eyes. They see over 3,000 images. Imagine trying to watch 3,000 six-sided TVs all at once!

Crop – flies have a second stomach. This one stores food ready to be sicked up and sucked up a few times until it's digested enough for the main stomach

Palps to taste your tea

Proboscis – think of a hairy drinking straw

Fly-brain quiz

You can win DOUBLE points if you don't use a calculator!

1 How fast can flies fly? Clue: = (10 – 2.76) km per hour.

2 A Roman anti-baldness cure involved smearing mashed-up fly paste on the head. How many flies were needed? Clue: add 92.76 flies to answer 1.

3 How many eggs can a female fly lay? Clue: add 400 eggs to answer 2.

4 How many flies can hatch in a dustbin? Clue: 3 x 60 flies.

5 How many flies did Beatrice White kill in a 1912 Swat the Fly Competition in Canada? Clue: add 513,360 flies to answer 4.

THWACK!

OOF!

APOLOGIES CAESAR, SOME ARE STILL WRIGGLING!

Answers:

1 7.24 You can escape from a swarm of angry flies if you run fast enough.

1 100. Don't try this on your dad. It didn't work!

2 500

3 30,000

4 543,360. Beatrice won $50. It was a pity she didn't kill flies in school. She could have been the class swat.

Sicking on your supper is bad enough – but then flies pee on it too. They also carry millions of bacteria and spread around 100 disgusting diseases. Mind you, if your house of horror is full of flies you could hire an ancient Egyptian human fly trap...

How to try a human fly remover

1 Pour a jug of milk over a slave's head.

2 Order them to stand in the corner.

VZZZZZZZZ!

WHAAAA!

3 When they're covered in flies they walk out of the house and take the flies with them!

MUNCHING MAGGOTS AND BEETLES

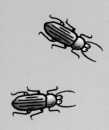

Scientists have found out where flies like to lay eggs. Their favourite places are…

Horse poo　　　**Human poo**　　　**Cow poo**　　　**Rotting vegetables and rubbish**

Hopefully you don't have giant poo piles in your home. But you'd best get rid of smelly rubbish – in a few days you could have millions of wriggling maggots. Maggots aren't fussy about where they live. Different species lurk in:

Horse's guts

THEY GET RIGHT UP MY NOSE…

YEAH – I HATE THEIR GUTS… BUT THEY SEEM TO LIKE MINE!

Sheep nostrils

Any kind of rotting flesh

Poo (again!)

CHEW!

The maggots burrow in their disgusting dinner and EAT IT. Then they form a pupa. Can you guess how a fly gets out of its pupa? Their head swells to break the case open. Just imagine your head got as big as a beach ball when you got up in the morning! I bet you'd get the day off school – you might even get a whole lifetime off school! Flies don't have long to enjoy being flies. Male flies live just 17 days and females 21 days – and less if you swat them!

Hmm – maggots sound dirty. I bet doctors hate them!

YOU'RE SQUASHING ME!

NOT NECESSARILY. HOSPITALS USE MAGGOTS TO REMOVE DISEASED FLESH. I'M THINKING OF TRYING A FEW ON MY IDIOT PATIENTS.

BORING DOCTOR NEWS

SAY GOODBYE TO WEEPING WOUNDS!

Are putrid gashes and unhealed bed sores making your life a bore? Come to the Maggot Memorial Hospital! Our little workers will gobble your dead flesh and bacteria. You're left with a nice clean wound that heals fast! *'I've got no scars and my bottom has never looked better!'* Satisfied patient

The only trouble is that the maggots itch as they nibble your putrid flesh. But they're only trying to help. One early fan of the maggot treatment was fifth-century saint Simon Stylitis. Saintly Simon was famous for sitting on top of a pillar for 39 years. He must have been fond of the high life. At one point in his career he got an ulcer and maggots moved in. The sensible saint left the maggots to munch in peace. He even put his little pals back in the wound when they fell off.

Oh yuck! Let's change the subject. Back in the Baron's putrid pantry the beetles are laying their eggs. Soon the loathsome larvae will gobble the Baron's food supplies.

Flour beetle

I EAT... OK, SO HOW DID YOU KNOW THAT? BUT I'LL TRY ANYTHING ONCE. GOT ANY CORNFLAKES?

Confused flour beetle

I AM NOT CONFUSED! HUMANS ARE CONFUSED BECAUSE THEY MUDDLE ME WITH THE RED RUST FLOUR BEETLE. WHAT YEAR IS IT? WHO DID I SAY I WAS?

Bacon beetle

I LOVE ... CHEESE. HA HA GOTCHA! YOU THOUGHT I WAS GOING TO SAY 'BACON' DIDN'T YOU? WELL, I LOVE BACON TOO AND I WOULDN'T SAY 'NO' TO A SMELLY DEAD MOUSE!

Biscuit beetle

BISCUITS AND FLOURY STUFF ARE BAD FOR YOU. SO IS POISON. BUT I'LL EAT THE LOT SO YOU DON'T HAVE TO!

ER, WHICH WAY TO THE NEXT PAGE?

SINISTER SPIDERS

If ugly bugs look set to take over your home – don't despair. Help is at hand!

There are more than 36,000 spider species. This one's the most common in homes. You might find it swimming in your soup or scaring your sister in the bath.

Instant expert: the house spider

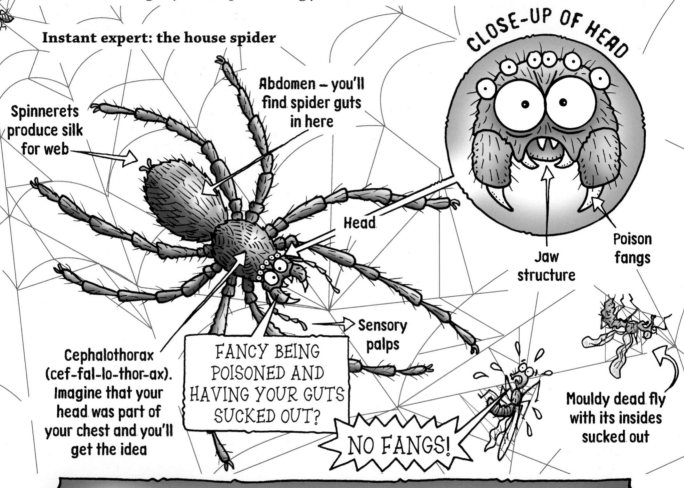

CLOSE-UP OF HEAD

Spinnerets produce silk for web

Abdomen – you'll find spider guts in here

Head

Jaw structure

Poison fangs

Little tube where spiders hide

Cephalothorax (cef-fal-lo-thor-ax). Imagine that your head was part of your chest and you'll get the idea

FANCY BEING POISONED AND HAVING YOUR GUTS SUCKED OUT?

Sensory palps

NO FANGS!

Mouldy dead fly with its insides sucked out

HORRIBLE HEALTH WARNING!

It's common in Europe and North America. If you live in parts of Australia you might share your home with a black spider. Bites from this spider can cause swelling and vomiting. So *don't* make friends with it!

Every horrible scientist knows that flies get stuck to spider webs. And then the spider grabs the fly and injects poison through its fearsome fangs. The victim can't move. The sinister spider vomits digestive juices over its living victim and slurps the soupy goo. But what about spider family life? Surely they have a caring side? Read on and find out!

House spider webs are horribly untidy

58

House spider family life - A report by PC Beetle

I called at the house spider residence after complaints that the Spiders were a 'problem family.' In response to my questions Mrs Spider admitted that she hadn't seen her husband since last autumn. 'He stayed for a bite,' she admitted. 'I might have eaten him by mistake.' According to Mrs Spider her husband died of natural causes. I am not so sure...

Mrs Spider told me that her babies were living with her. 'They don't get on too well – in fact they keep eating each other. I'm glad they're moving to their own webs' she said. She then asked me to stick around for supper. At this point I tried to leave but I couldn't...

BET YOU NEVER KNEW!

This is happy families by Australian social spider standards. The spider mum lets her babies suck her blood. When she's too weak to move, they sick up digestive juices and turn her into mush and slurp up the revolting remains. I bet the babies say 'our mum makes a lovely tea!'

Teacher's tea-break teaser

Bang on the staffroom door. When it opens, show your teacher your pet spider and ask...

WHY DOESN'T BERTIE STICK TO HIS WEB?

YARRRGH!

STAFFR

Answer:

Scientists have been arguing about this for years. Even if your teacher knows the answer, it will take her ages to explain. Basically, not all web strands are sticky and the sensible spiders walk on the non-sticky threads. If they do tread on a blob of glue they free themselves with the claws at the end of their horribly hairy legs.

WHAT'S BURPING IN YOUR BATHROOM?

By now you might be thinking that your home has quite a few hidden horrors. But the bathroom is where things get horribly horrible. I mean – just look at the Baron's bathroom!

Belly button fluff is a moist mix of dead skin cells, bacteria and clothes fibres.

Wet towels ooze with delicious dead skin cells. Bacteria love it.

Demodex mite hiding here – find out why on page 63.

Condensation on windows makes a lovely moist home for mould.

Soap removes grease and germs – you can check out how on page 62.

Are there hairs in your bathroom? Maybe it's because people brush their hair in front of the bathroom mirror. Hairs grow about 5 cm per year and fall out after three years or 15 cm.

GO AWAY!

YEAH, BOG OFF!

Drip of pee on toilet seat. Pee gets filtered from your blood by your kidneys. It's low in germs when it comes out of your body. But bacteria in pee breed quickly – with smelly results.

Toilet rim is a favourite bacteria hideout.

Water in toilet brush holder is full of floating poo particles and bacteria.

This shy silverfish isn't a fish. It's an insect that lives in damp corners and guzzles glue and mould from wet wallpaper.

Fungus growing on base of bath mat.

Interesting mould munching the shower curtain.

Here's what the shrinking scientists find in the Baron's bathroom. Are there similar horrors lurking on your lino?

Cute little amoeba exploring a toothbrush. This harmless protist munches mouth bacteria. It's waiting to leap into someone's mouth.

This scabby used sticking plaster is fascinating. Let's ask the shrinking scientists to take a closer look...

Bathroom dust is full of dead skin cells and mites.

The shrinking scientists in... All stuck up!

TINY PORES IN THE PLASTIC LET IN AIR AND SPEED UP HEALING.

THE PAD SOAKS UP BLOOD AND PUS.

I CAN'T SEE ANY PAWS!

THE GLUE HELPS STICK THE PLASTER TO THE SKIN.

I'M IN A STICKY SITUATION!

LOOK AT THIS FASCINATING SCAB...

A BLOOD PROTEIN CALLED FIBRIN FORMED A NET OF FIBRES.

THE NET CAUGHT PLATELETS AND RED BLOOD CELLS.

IT'S A CLOT!

IT TAKES ONE TO KNOW ONE!

WEIRD WASHING

Every time you have a wash you're actually doing really crazy chemistry...
Read on if you don't believe me!

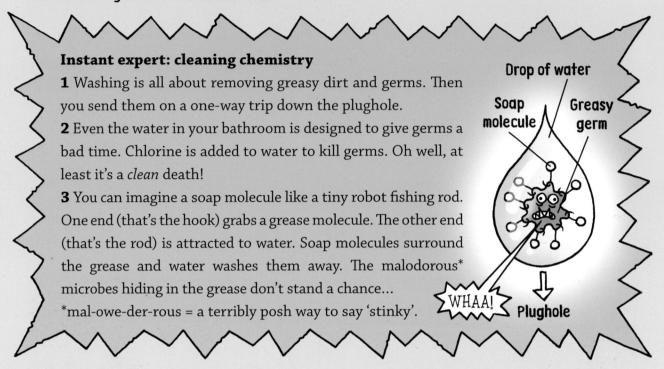

Instant expert: cleaning chemistry

1 Washing is all about removing greasy dirt and germs. Then you send them on a one-way trip down the plughole.

2 Even the water in your bathroom is designed to give germs a bad time. Chlorine is added to water to kill germs. Oh well, at least it's a *clean* death!

3 You can imagine a soap molecule like a tiny robot fishing rod. One end (that's the hook) grabs a grease molecule. The other end (that's the rod) is attracted to water. Soap molecules surround the grease and water washes them away. The malodorous* microbes hiding in the grease don't stand a chance...

*mal-owe-der-rous = a terribly posh way to say 'stinky'.

Drop of water
Soap molecule
Greasy germ
WHAA!
Plughole

Chances are your bathroom is full of bottles and tubes of strange substances. They're all designed to make your skin cleaner and nicer-smelling. Here are some hideous historic skincare remedies that we found in the Baron's bathroom. They sound weird but people really did use them!

Heritage Health Care

Want to look pale and interesting? Try ye modern eighteenth-century way with Wonder Water Skin Bleach! Guaranteed results every time!

The small print:
Poisonous mercury flakes away your skin and the poison makes your teeth fall out. But cheer up, you'll look deathly pale ... when you're dead.

YIPPEE - NO NORE DENTIFF'S BILLS!

TRY TRADITIONAL ARABIAN CAMEL PEE SHAMPOO — it's a wee bit different!

IT MAKES YOUR HAIR WAVY.

BUT DON'T GET THE HUMP IF IT DOESN'T WORK.

Traditional Elizabethan face wash

You'll feel playful as a puppy with puppy pee face wash. All natural ingredients and there's plenty more inside the puppy!

MANUFACTURERS GUARANTEE
So you're not happy? Oh dear — time to go! If you find us we'll give you a free bar of soap. Made to an eighteenth-century recipe, it contains 100% natural pig poo!

Ye Puppy Pee Potion

Once you're washed you'll want to get dry. And that brings us to that creature on the bath towel. The demodex mite is a revolting relative of the dust mites on page 72. It hides in the pits of your eyelashes and scoffs bacteria.

The mites spread when you share a towel. Or when you touch foreheads with someone. And that's why your mites are related to the mites on your family. Just think – there's a family living on your family's eyelashes. And none of your family have ever seen them!

Baby mites go off looking for a new home and more bacteria to guzzle. They love oily skin because more microbes live there. Isn't that sweet?

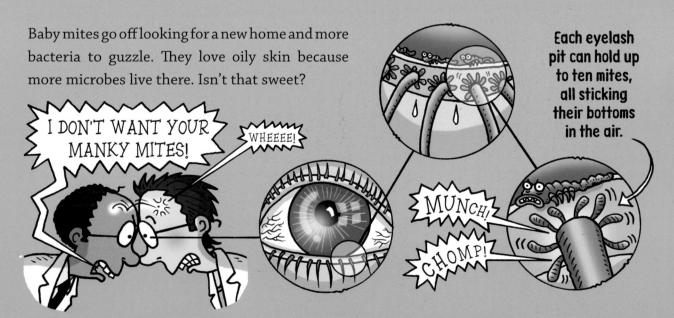

I DON'T WANT YOUR MANKY MITES!

WHEEEE!

Each eyelash pit can hold up to ten mites, all sticking their bottoms in the air.

MUNCH!

CHOMP!

THE TOILET OF DOOM

Even the scariest bath-time can't compete with the unspeakable terrors in your toilet!

Mind you, things used to be a lot worse. Before flush loos, toilets were built over cesspits. Cleaning or 'raking' the putrid pit wasn't popular. In 1326 Richard the Raker fell in his own cesspit and sank out of sight.

ME THINKS MASTER RICHARD BE ASKING FOR YE BOG ROLL!

In 1845 twenty women prisoners at Exeter Castle, England were locked in one cell. The floor gave way. They fell in the cesspit and five drowned in pongy poo. So the flush toilet just *had* to be a good invention…

Dare you discover … how your toilet works?

You will need:

A drinking straw (It needs to be a wide one with a bendy section)

A glass filled to the brim with water

A sink

What you do:

1 Place the bent end of the straw in the water.

2 Suck water into the straw until it's completely filled with water. Then, quickly take the straw out of your mouth and hold the end low over the sink.

AIR

SPLOOSH!

NO, JUNIOR, IT WOULDN'T MAKE IT MORE LIKE A TOILET IF YOU ADDED SOME CHOCOLATE RAISINS!

You should find:

As long as the other end stays underwater, the water flows up the straw. Water molecules are drawn together – remember that fact from page 50? Air pushes on the water surface and shoves the water up the straw. It's called the siphon (si-fon) effect. When you flush your toilet, you pour water into the bowl. The siphon effect pushes water (and poo) round the bend.

What's more those flying poo droplets can land on your toothbrush! This really is true, but don't panic. I said DON'T! These germs don't do much harm. In fact scientists think they work like a vaccination by getting your body's defences used to bacteria. This helps you to fight nastier microbes – so flushing the loo's good for you!

Poo is 75% water and 12.5% bacteria. The rest is the food you can't digest and snotty mucus. This is useless, which is why your body gets rid of it. But some dodgy doctors found a use for it. Here's a seventeenth-century remedy that you can try if you're completely stupid.

It doesn't work – but who cares? You'll feel so sick that you'll forget about what made you ill!

FREAKY FUNGI

You may think your bathroom is a room with a bath in it. But to the foul fungi family it's a restaurant oozing with tasty titbits. And that includes your toenails.

Instant expert: Foul fungi

1 Fungi experts (they're known as mycologists*) reckon there could be one million fungi species. Most are unknown to science. Fungi feed using tubes called hyphae (hi-fee) that drill into their dinner and produce digestive juices. The foul fungus slurps up its soupy supper.

Mouldy apple core

SLURP!

2 A fungus grows a fruiting body and makes millions of airborne spores.

3 The mushrooms on your pizza are fruiting bodies of the Agaricus (a-gari-cus) fungus. But not all fruiting bodies are tasty. Poisonous toadstools are fruiting bodies that you shouldn't sample unless you want to be a dead body.

Mushroom

Toadstool

*mi-col-lo-gists

Foul fungi can pop up all over your home. There might be...

NOT AGAIN! (SEE PAGE 38)

Penicillium fungi scoff bread and fruit. Remember them from page 49?

Wet rot fungus gobble wet woodwork such as your floorboards.

WHAA!

Dry rot fungi spread from damp to dry wood. They can bore through brick and eat your home.

MUNCH!

NIBBLE!

Some Penicillium fungi scoff soap.

If a house isn't draughty, water vapour from cooking, washing and spitty breath will condense on cool surfaces. It makes a happy home for moulds. Your bathroom is a mouldy paradise. Black moulds guzzle paint, plaster, paper and dust. And they'll eat your carpets and wallpaper for dessert. Mind you, if that sounds foul, at least they don't eat you. Unlike these guys...

Lucky Lifestyles Weekly

Dr Grimgrave's Health Page

Tell Dr G your problems and he'll make you feel a whole lot worse. Just DON'T call him 'Doc' and don't ask for a home visit!

Dear Dr Grimgrave,

I've got itchy feet. ITCH! My doctor says it's tinea pedis - is this the end of me? I've got to know the worst - I'm sweating in my socks!

Mia Toebad

Dear Ms Toebad,

Sweaty socks caused your problem. Tinea fungi attack skin between your toes. The results can be interesting – scaly peeling skin and thick yellow toenails. Treat it with medical ointment and don't share your sweaty socks!

PS Make sure you change them before you come into my surgery!

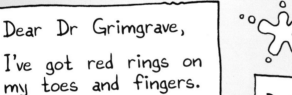

Dear Dr Grimgrave,

I've got red rings on my toes and fingers.

You've got to help! I feel like I'm growing in circles!

M E Itchin

Dear Mr Itchin,

Sounds like ringworm to me! This is the result of tinea fungi spreading in a circle as it feeds on keratin in your skin. It's treatable with a medical ointment.

PS It's nothing to do with worms

Dear Doc,

I've got fungus in my hair. Am I turning into a toadstool?

Ida Brushett

PS Can I have a home visit?

HELP!

Dear Ms Brushett,

You have a species of tinea fungus. It can be treated with special medicines. Meanwhile don't lend your brush to anyone.

PS Don't call me 'Doc'!
PPS NO YOU CAN'T!

WHAT'S SNOOZING
IN YOUR BED?

Feeling worn out? Well, if you're ready to crash you'd best do it now. Once you've read this chapter you'll probably get nightmares! The shrinking scientists are bravely exploring Monster Boy's spooky bedroom …

1 Clothes moth wants to turn the Monster Boy's pants into a fashion disaster zone (see page 70).

2 Peckish mosquito waits patiently for supper (that's blood, by the way – see page 74).

3 Mouldy mattress soaks up 600 ml of Monster Boy's sweat per night.

4 Pfwoar! Monster Boy's pants are full of skin flakes and bacteria and revolting poo particles. I'm surprised they don't walk out the door on their own!

5 Greasy fingerprints = late-night snack for bacteria.

6 The rotten remains of a late night snack. Lucky the cockroaches haven't found this!

7 Bedbug thirsting for Monster Boy's blood.

8 Disgusting dust

9 Floorboards soak moisture all day and dry out at night. As they dry they make ghostly creaks to scare Monster Boy witless. (That's even more witless than he is now!)

Monster Boy's disgusting pants started life as fluffy seed cases of the cotton bush. The fluffy fibres have been twisted into yarn and woven to make a soft-textured fabric. And I hate to spoil things by telling you that the fibres easily fray and leave a hole in the pants.

MUNCH! MUNCH! Hey, what's that sound? Oh yes, I nearly forgot – there's a carpet beetle in the bedroom! Did you spot her? She's laid her eggs and her larvae want to eat Monster Boy's carpet…

The Carpet Beetle Good Hotel Guide
THE BEDROOM DE-LUXE ★★★★
(room for 100 eggs)

The stay of a lifetime! In fact we want to stay for the rest of our lifetime! My 100 grubs loved the carpet bed and breakfast! Baron Frankenstein was SO welcoming. He greeted us with a song that sounded like, 'ARGGGGH! Look at my carpet!' Then he started chewing the carpet with us!

BET YOU NEVER KNEW!
There's a worse carpet beetle relative. Some skin beetles like nothing better than stripping flesh from the bones of dead animals. Museums once used them to clean up animal skeletons for display. But nowadays only mad scientists like the Baron use them!

STOP! IT TICKLES!

THE CREEPY CLOTHES SHOW

That creepy clothes moth really was planning to do terrible things to Monster Boy's pants. We asked ace reporter Randall Scandall to check her out...

The Horrible Science Interview
with Randall Scandal

RS: Can have I have a word?

CM: Can't stop, darling. I've just laid my eggs and I'm frantic! My larvae are putting on a fashion show!

RS: What's their favourite label?

CM: Only the best wool and natural fibres, darling. And they just have to be dirty! Clean is just so-o-o last year! The humans add the dirt. All that lovely grease and skin cells and bacteria! My larvae are working on Monster Boy's pants...

RS: What are they doing?

CM: Holes, darling. They are definitely in this season. Aren't they fabulous? The larvae shed their skins – poor darlings. It's so hard being a larva – you just can't find a skin to fit you!

RS: What do they do next?

CM: They spin a cocoon. In a few weeks, they'll hatch as totally gorgeous supermodel moths like me. And then it's show time!

RS: Show time?

CM: Show off the holes in your pants time... Oh well, can't stop – must fly!

RS: Grr... WHO ATE MY TROUSERS?

Two species of clothes moth nibble your underwear. There's the common clothes moth (I bet it burps a lot – that's a common habit) and the brown clothes moth. Can any of you science geniuses work out what colour the brown clothes moth is?

BET YOU NEVER KNEW!

Talking about cotton clothing, archaeologists have found ancient cotton cloth. The ancient fabric from Mexico is 7,000 years old. I hope Monster Boy's pants are a bit more recent!

Clothes moths like natural fibres like cotton and wool. You can see the difference between natural and artificial fibres under the microscope...

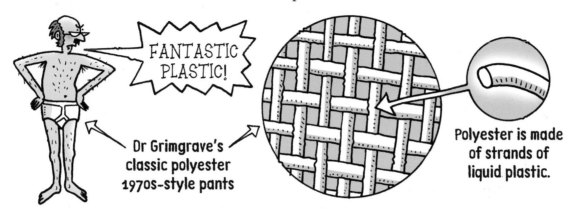

FANTASTIC PLASTIC!

Dr Grimgrave's classic polyester 1970s-style pants

Polyester is made of strands of liquid plastic.

The plastic is spun fast and the strands are spun out and allowed to dry. In the 1840s British inventor Louis Schwabe used a similar method to spin glass fibres. I guess you could make glass pants but they might shatter if you ate too many beans. Now that *would* be a SHATTERING EXPERIENCE!

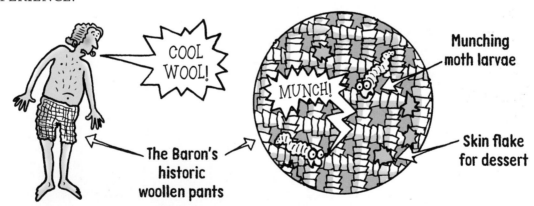

COOL WOOL!

MUNCH!

Munching moth larvae

Skin flake for dessert

The Baron's historic woollen pants

Seen through a microscope, wool looks like hair. And that's not surprising because wool is sheep hair. Like your hair, it's scaly. And like your hair, wool feels nice and warm because it traps warm air close to your skin. No wonder moth larvae find wool toasty!

And talking about skin flakes for dessert, there's a creature that's been crawling in our footsteps all day. It's lurking in your living room and eyeballing your eyelashes. Now we've tracked it down to its favourite hideaway. It's on the next page!

THE MITEY MITE

There's one creature that creeps from every creepy corner of your home. I'm talking about the disgusting dust mites and they're especially at home in your bed! The shrinking scientists are exploring Monster Boy's pillow…

The shrinking scientists in… Pillow fright!

The Cheyletus is known as the 'cannibal mite'. What a brilliant name! You can tell your mum that you can't go to bed because cannibals live there. But there isn't much point. Even if you got rid of every dust mite, more would crawl in from your carpet. And would you *really* want to sleep on a frozen pillow? Anyway, dust mites are scientifically fascinating!

Three scientifically fascinating mite facts

1 The scientific name for one dust mite species is dermatophagoides pteronyssinus (that's der-mo-tof-fag-goy-des terro-ny-sin-us). It's Greek for 'skin-eating feather-stalker'. Obviously scientists don't like dust mites!

2 There are some places that you expect to find mites. And some you don't. Can you believe that scientists have found mites living in...

In fact, they're *everywhere*. You can find hundreds of mite species in a few metres of forest.

3 Many mite species live on crops. This is a problem because they munch the crops. In 2001 the South American green mite was scrunching the African cassava crop. But scientists brought in a Brazilian mite to guzzle the grisly green gangsters.

Could you be a dust mite expert?

This quiz is so ridiculously simple even a dust mite could do it. All you have to do is match the awful answers to the queasy questions!

QUEASY QUESTIONS

1 How many mite species are there?

2 Here's half a teaspoonful of dust.

How many mites are hiding in it?

3 And how many mite poos?

4 Roughly how many mites share your bed with you?

AWFUL ANSWERS:

a) About 1,000.

b) About one million

c) Over 48,000 (or many times more)

d) Around 250,000

Answers:
1c), 2a), 3d), 4b).

THE MEASLY MOSQUITO

Oh look - it's the most evil, horrible, monstrous, dangerous beast on the planet! And it's in your bedroom! This must be the ultimate horror!

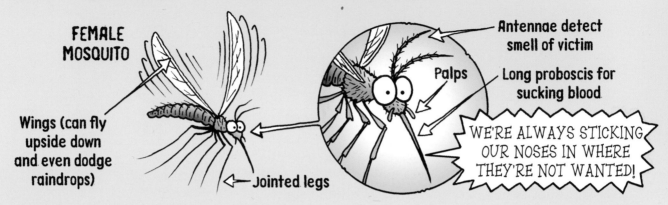

FEMALE MOSQUITO

Antennae detect smell of victim

Palps

Long proboscis for sucking blood

Wings (can fly upside down and even dodge raindrops)

Jointed legs

WE'RE ALWAYS STICKING OUR NOSES IN WHERE THEY'RE NOT WANTED!

Mosquito larvae lurk in water scoffing algae (tiny plants) or bacteria. After a few days as a pupa, they hatch. Then they've got a week to mate, lay eggs and die. And that's when the bloodsucking begins...

MOZZIE WORLD MAGAZINE

In this month's magazine

* Celebrity bite stories (they spill their secrets and we spill their blood!)

* Blood banks - are they such a good idea?

* Cooking page - make a colourful blood cocktail!

* Your stars - some of you are going to suck blood this week and most of you will die.

PARTY TIME!

How to find a perfect meal
by Mozzie Buzz

It's OK for those lazy males to sip plant juice all day but we girls need our energy. Laying eggs is hard work! That's why a girl has got to have blood. Luckily humans lay on a free supply for us. All we have to do party on down at dawn and dusk. Go for their carbon-dioxide breath and don't forget, girls - the sweaty ones taste best!* Simply slice their skin, get stuck in with your drinking tube and you're in business! Don't forget a dribble of anti-clotting spit - blood clots can be such a bore! And do remember the golden rule - IF YOU GET SPOTTED YOU'LL GET SWATTED!

*It's true

DELICIOUS!

SLURRP!

BET YOU NEVER KNEW!

Scientists can block nerve signals from the mosquito's stomach that tell its brain when it's full. The mozzie sucks blood until it explodes with messy results!

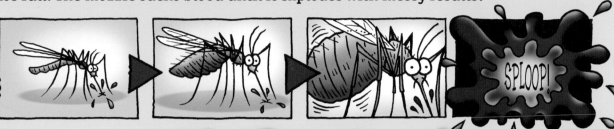

SPLOOP!

It's the deadly diseases that make the mosquito a killer. In the 2000s diseases such as malaria and yellow fever spread by mosquitoes killed two million people per year. Please don't scream too loud! Most bites leave nothing more than an itchy spot caused by an allergic reaction to mozzie spit. And mozzies in cooler countries don't spread these diseases.

Could you be a mosquito scientist?

How did Dutch scientist Bart Knols prove that one mosquito species likes to attack your feet?

a) He gave them stinky cheese to sniff.

b) He let the mosquitoes attack scientists dressed in their underpants.

YARRRRRGH!

Answer:

b) The biting blighters went for the boffins' feet. There's half a point for

a) because Bart proved that the mozzies were attracted by stinky cheese!

It's time to sleep. But wait, I forgot to tell you about bedbugs! They're quite rare, but they once lived in cracks in bedrooms and crept out to suck blood when their victims were asleep. Goodnight and hope the bugs don't bite!

KEEP THE NOISE DOWN – YOU'LL WAKE HIM UP!

SUCK!

SLURP!

ZZZZZZZZZ

Is your home that bad? Well, I bet it has a few of the horrible things in this book. But hopefully not *all* of them!

So how does that make you feel? Scared? Upset? Queasy? No longer safe in your own home? Hopefully not! I think there's nothing wrong with a little mess, a little untidiness, even the odd spider. They make a home feel like home. And don't you think it's the tatty, messy, scruffy bits of your home that make it your special place?

And here's another reason why every home needs a few hidden horrors... Did you notice how much science there was in this book? A lot of people think that science stops at their front door. But a lot of people are wrong. Science actually STARTS in the home. After all it's where the coolest science can be found – all you need is imagination! And I guess that's the real point of this book. Science isn't about lessons – it's all around you. Especially the horrible bits!

GRUESOME GLOSSARY

Acid – a chemical that dissolves other substances when mixed with water. Including human bodies.

Allergy – when your body reacts to a harmless substance like pollen. You might get a snotty nose or sore skin.

Atom – tiny balls of matter. They form you and everything else in the universe. Each atom has a nucleus surrounded by a cloud of electrons. This nucleus is nothing to do with a cell nucleus.

Bacteria (one is a bacterium) – are life-forms with one cell. You'll find bacteria in every disgusting place you can think of. Plus a few places you wouldn't want to think of!

Cell – plants and animals are made of cells. The cell nucleus has chromosomes made of DNA. This molecule is a chemical code to build your body. It orders the cell to build proteins.

PLANT CELLS

Chitin – a substance made of chains of sugar molecules. It turns up in yucky places such as cockroach armour, spider skin and fungus feeding tubes.

CHITIN ARMOUR

Chromosome – lengths of DNA found in the cell nucleus. Each species has a certain number of chromosomes. You've got 46. Sounds impressive? Not really! Your dog has 78.

Condensation – when molecules in a gas cool and form a liquid. It's the opposite of evaporation.

Digestion – when digestive juices in your guts break your food into small molecules. These molecules pass into your blood and feed your body cells.

DNA – a chemical code to build your body. It orders the cell to build proteins.

Electrons – particles that make an electric force. They're usually whizzing around atoms.

Evaporation – when a liquid warms and turns to gas. The molecules float away, taking heat with them.

Gland – a body bit that makes a substance. No prizes for guessing what your spit glands make!

DRIBBLE!

Molecule – two or more atoms bonded together.

Osmosis – the way water gets into a cell. The cell wall has tiny holes or pores. Water molecules can get through them but larger molecules in the cell are too big to escape though the holes. So the cell gets a nice drink and its insides stay inside!

Parasite – a loathsome life-form that lives off another species and harms its host. Some parasites have parasites – for example dog fleas have gut protists. That's so (NOT) tragic!

IT MAKES ME HOPPING MAD!

Platelet – tiny blood cells without a nucleus. You need them for clotting but they're nothing to do with dinner plates.

PLATELET   PLATE

Pollen – imagine a micro-balloon full of DNA. Its mission is to find a flower of the same species and grow into a seed. Hay fever is when the pollen wafts up your nose and causes an allergic reaction.

Protein – molecule made of amino acids. They're folded in complex ways that give boffins headaches. Each of your cells contains millions of proteins.

Protist – it's not you complaining about being sent to bed early – that's a *protest*. Protists usually have one cell with a cell nucleus and live in water. The best-known protist is the amoeba.

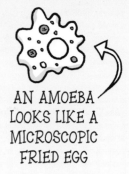

AN AMOEBA LOOKS LIKE A MICROSCOPIC FRIED EGG

Proton – particle in the nucleus of an atom. A proton's electric force helps to hold the atom together.

Species – type of plant or animal.

LADYBIRD

I'M A SPECIES OF BEETLE.

Vaccination – your blood contains billions of white blood cells ready to kill germs. This is your immune system. Vaccination gives your body weak or dead germs to get it used to fighting that disease.

Virus – DNA in a protein case. It can only multiply inside a living cell. Which is bad news for us.

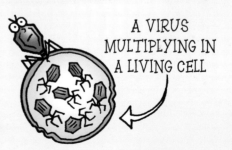

A VIRUS MULTIPLYING IN A LIVING CELL

YEAST CELLS MULTIPLYING

Yeast – type of fungi with one cell. It's found in soil all over the world.

HORRIBLE INDEX